AuthorHouse™
1663 Liberty Drive, Suite 200
Bloomington, IN 47403
www.authorhouse.com
Phone: 1-800-839-8640

First published by AuthorHouse   4/14/2008

ISBN: 978-1-4343-7492-9 (sc)
ISBN: 978-1-4343-7493-6 (hc)
ISBN: 978-1-4343-7494-3 (e)

Library of Congress Control Number: 2008903256

Printed in the United States of America
Bloomington, Indiana

This book is printed on acid-free paper.

Military Logistics Made Easy

Concept, Theory, and Execution

by

LTC James H. Henderson
"Cotton", USA (Ret.)

Preface

You already know that logistics is hard, it should not be, but it just is. The key components to supply and movement are the same as they were in the days of George Washington's and Nathanael Greene consisting of *receive, store, issue,* and *move.* It should be that simple. You receive, store, and issue the items, and when its time to move them, you cube out a wagon just as you cube out an airplane; you weigh out before you cube out. The problem is that it is much easier said than done. Bottom line: it just is not that simple. There are too many moveable parts where the synergy of the operation could provide a scenario where the combined requirements needed to sustain a theater are greater than the sum of their individual effects or capabilities. Let us review a typical go to war scenario. We deploy to an area of operation and begin to build combat power consisting of supplies, equipment and personnel. We get to a point when combat operations begin and we use stocks to support the operation. Now we are still bringing supplies, equipment, and personnel into theater as we are conducting combat operations, but it is a slow process. As combat operations continue, we gain land and physical resources like roads, buildings, and airports just to name a few, which begins to develop our logistical distribution network. Then, just as quickly as combat operations developed they stop and we are left with trying to create a logistical distribution network quickly that will support the new theater of operation. The picture I have painted is what happens during every conflict or war in the beginning and then the years of a campaign leave the logistical personnel dealing with an immature theater, and it is only over time that will enough supplies, equipment, and personnel be deployed to transform it into a fully mature theater.

This book outlines some of these logistical components and their doctrinal relationship to the operation, as well as provides some new ideas. The chapters are formatted in a fashion that offer the reader the doctrinal concept that the operation or function is based on, and then presents new theories on how to better execute the logistical function or capability as it relates to the operation. The book is organized into the following sections consisting of *Structure, Accounting, Planning, Execution,* and *Situational Awareness.* Each section has a series of chapters that discuss the purpose and how they are utilized in the support of logistical operations. My goal is to discuss those hard logistical topics and their conception to improve the general knowledge and understanding on *"why it happens"*, and *"how we can improve the outcome*". Of course, these are just my theories, but over my twenty-years plus experiences, they have assisted me in my execution of logistical operations. I have taken and adapted some chapters from my previous two books (*The Process of Military Distribution Management; A Guide to Assist Military and Civilian Logisticians in Linking Commodities and Movement*, and *Logistics in Support of Disaster Relief*) to assist in the explanations of certain theories, and how to best execute the functions.

Contents

Figures

Tables

Structure

Chapter 1

Battle Rhythm

Concept

Battle rhythm is the process where the staff levels provide situational awareness that allow commanders to make timely decisions. Battle rhythm is the synchronization of logistical activities and processes in their support of tactical operations. Successful battle rhythm implies the synergism of procedures, processes, technologies, individual activities and collective actions at the tactical and operational levels to facilitate military operations.

Theory and Execution

In my opinion, the success of any logistical support operations is the quick and timely interjection of a staff battle rhythm to develop the bases for the subordinate unit's execution to be structured. Battle rhythm reflects the operational-tempo of the tactical operation it is supporting, and must change within an individual battle, campaign, or throughout the process of a war. There can be more than one battle rhythm dependent on the different levels of war, which I discuss in detail in this section, chapter 3, Levels of Logistics. There can be more than one battle rhythm supporting an operation, and they can be related due to a subordinate unit relationship, or mutual sustainment and support forward. The key is to nest the different battle rhythms within the process to facilitate a smooth transition, and not to create obstacles and delays within the operation.

This is also easier said than done, but to be able to achieve success creating a workable and manageable process a staff must know their mission relationship and the key ingredients making up their battle rhythm. For this example, I will use logistical support operations, but it could be used with tactical maneuver operations just as easily depending on the mission and type of unit. The first ingredient is *structure* consisting of the migration of a maturing logistical battlefield, the different levels of logistical support, and their linkage to one another. The second item is *accounting* relating to logistical reporting that identifies requirements, projections, and forecasts that gives visibility on critical shortages, readiness, and offers input to the common operating picture (COP). The combatant forces provide the operational-tempo, but it is depicted within the support battle rhythm in two areas: 1) the reporting cycle, and 2) the sustainment cycle. The reporting cycle leads us to our third component *planning,* in which the information is the basis of preparation and planning for future, as well as ongoing sustainment and support operations. The sustainment cycle leads to the fourth component *execution* that nests the staffs planning and management functions to the subordinate unit's implementation of the actual mission. The fifth element is *situational awareness* where the mechanics of information management and the procedures a staff utilizes to process input and output that supports a common operating picture (COP). If all five components are nested and implemented correctly the battle rhythm will ultimately provide synergy within the operation.

The following chapters within this book discuss in detail the different components to provide a better understanding in their relationship, or support to one another. It is because the battle rhythm is the key, and it is then we need to understand different functions that are required to develop a successful logistical support operations battle rhythm.

Chapter 2

Logistical Support Operations

Concept

Full Spectrum Operations is the name used when you are talking about the Army's operational concept. The concept addresses the wide range of conflicts linked to military missions. This operational concept is the foundation for all Army doctrine.

Full spectrum operations are comprised of offensive, defensive, stability, and support operations. Different types of missions in any environment require preparation and training to successfully conduct any of these operations:

- *Offensive operations* pertain to destroying or defeating an enemy. The purpose is to achieve victory.

- *Defensive operations* crush an enemy attack, economize forces, or provide time for offensive operations, and allow a counteroffensive to regain the initiative.

- *Stability operations* support and protect national interests in response to crisis, and promote a stable environment.

- *Support operations* support civil authorities, foreign or domestic, in response to a crisis. Forces operate under federal agencies and operate under U.S. law, to include the Posse Comitatus and Stafford Acts.

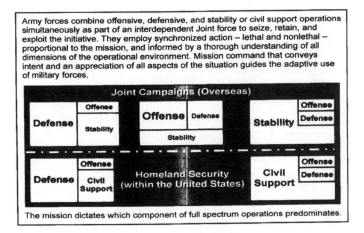

Army forces combine offensive, defensive, and stability or civil support operations simultaneously as part of an interdependent Joint force to seize, retain, and exploit the initiative. They employ synchronized action – lethal and nonlethal – proportional to the mission, and informed by a thorough understanding of all dimensions of the operational environment. Mission command that conveys intent and an appreciation of all aspects of the situation guides the adaptive use of military forces.

The mission dictates which component of full spectrum operations predominates.

Full Spectrum Operations [1]

So in review, the doctrinal concept of Full Spectrum Operations consist of four phases, and under those phases or categories are different types of military operations that relates to the four phases:

- Offensive operations relate to military operations that try to gain the initiative. Examples are operations such as Movement to Contact, Attack, Exploitation, and Pursuit. These are considered operations that gain objectives.

- Defensive operations relate to military operations that try to provide time, or regain the initiative, for example, operations such as Area Defense, Mobile Defense, and Retrograded Operation.

- Stability operations relate to military operations that try to promote a stable environment, for example operations such as Peace Operations (OPNS), Foreign Internal Defense, Security Assistance, Humanitarian & Civic Assistance, Support to Insurgences, Combating Terrorism, Noncombatant Evacuation OPNS, Arms Control, and Show of Force.

- Support operations relate to military operations that try to support civil authorities consisting of Domestic Support OPNS, Foreign Humanitarian Assistance, Relief OPNS, Support to Incidents Involving WMD, Support to Civil Law Enforcement, Community Assistance.

---

[1] Army Doctrine Update #1, 24 February 2007, 2

In addition, the two types of Logistical Support Operations that sustain the phases are Maneuver and Sustainment Operations. Maneuver operations mainly support offense and defense, and toward the tail end of defense, there is then a time that an operational pose occurs and sustainment operations begin. This is a good lead-in to the problem at hand. In my opinion, there are additional logistical support operations that are not identified.

Theory and Execution

As stated above, there is a need to identify additional logistical support operations, and by not identifying these additional operations, the logistic personnel may not really understand the migration of a maturing logistical battlefield, which requires a different battle rhythm in supporting and gauging the operational tempo of the distribution network.

I began to think of this theory because of what I observed during a trip I made to Balad, Iraq in October 2006. The soldiers down range said to me that they wanted to be able to conduct, *"trend analysis"* with the data complied within the logistical reporting tool we were developing. Trend analysis? I had been in two combat theaters and never heard the words *"trend analysis"*, but then neither one had lasted this long. I have heard the words used in garrison, but the battlefield had not migrated to a complete static environment to say it has matured to that extent. I could also tell the operational tempo had slowed down to some degree than when I was there before. I remembered it had been two years since I was stationed there during the tail end of OIF I, and II calendar year 2004. During that period, the president declared that the ground war (offensive and defensive) phase of operations (maneuver) was complete and we then moved into the stability operational phase (sustainment). Throughout that period, the operational tempo was high with two distribution movement boards being conducted daily just to keep sustainment requirements moving within a 72-hour cycle. The reason for this effect was obvious to me due to the fact that the distribution network was very immature at that time. The main explanations were the limited: available logistical lines of communication (LOC) into theater, resources consisting of force protection platforms, movement platforms (military and commercial), automation enablers (integrators and mobile tracking devices), available air in and outside of theater, as well as commodities forward. All of these conditions forced the staff to intensively manage logistical support operations just to maintain sustainment requirements forward to the five regions in Iraq. However, now I am witnessing a staff battle rhythm completely different in sense of urgency and priorities. The questions at hand were simple: *"why was this happening"*, and *"what was causing it to happen"*, to alter the operational tempo in such a manner. The answer was straightforward to me. The distribution network had matured, but what had caused this was not so simple, because there was not just one thing that changed this battle rhythm, but a series of events occurring which effected the maturity of the logistical battlefield. When I was there Logistical Support Area (LSA) Anaconda, Balad, Iraq was a main sustainment hub, with only one mature supporting LOC coming into country from the south, and two others are just being established from the north and west. Now we find LSA Anaconda is a reserve, and sustainment commodities have been built-up forward creating regional sustainment hubs, as well as having three mature supply routes to support the area of operation. Second reason, there is only one distribution board a day and really it is only confirming the scheduled movement times. It seems to me that there is now enough force protection and sustainment support platforms to balance maintenance, crew rest, and the sustainment cycle that gives the process some continuity and certainty, so the cycles do not have to be adjusted as frequently as they did in the past. Third, there is expected air in and out of the area of operations not only at LSA Anaconda, but also at the forward regional sustainment hubs. Lastly, more automation enablers have been established within the area of operations providing predictable logistical situational awareness. So let us review the key elements that occurred to create the maturity of the distribution network and initiated the establishment of a different battle rhythm:

1. Created regional sustainment hubs
2. Provided additional supply routes
3. Continuity in the resources
4. More automation enablers

These four factors lead me to believe that an operational pose has take place, and we have moved from sustainment operations to what I call management operations. This is where the distribution network has matured to the extent that the sustainment operational tempo has slowed in its intensity thus providing more time for the staff to analyze and assess the logistical posture. Now do not get me wrong, the combat operational tempo has not changed, but because of the maturity of the distribution network over time the logistical posture has moved to the right. This you will see if you look at the four types of military operation (Full Spectrum Operations) on a sliding scale (See Figure 1; Logistical Support Operations Sliding Scale). As you can see from the diagram, during the offensive and defensive phases, we are mainly under maneuver operations. But towards the end of defensive and the beginning of stability operations, we see an operational pose and the logistician moves into the sustainment operation phase. The critical point occurs during stability operations when the intensity of the operational tempo stabilizes to such a point that the staff and supporting unit's battle rhythm can adjust to allow for more detailed commodity management. Identifying exactly when this trigger point occurs or to what extent the distribution network has matured will depend on the duration of the military operation. But it does occur as pointed out previously.

I also must submit that as military operations draw down and supporting units redeploy, the distribution network will decrease in maturity causing a reverse effect in the staff's battle rhythm. Example: If they retrograde units and equipment leaving a situation where their LOC could be overextended and thus units and equipment were not systematically redeployed, then we could then very easily see the operational tempo and staff battle rhythm intensify as it did in the sustainment operation phase. There is one additional situation, and that is if combat operations increase as we begin to withdraw forces then this could also cause a reversal in the logistical support operational phases. Both of the scenarios point out that some sort of reversal in logistical support operations are apparent and that staff elements must be aware of the changing operational tempo to predict and adjust their battle rhythm accordingly.

In addition, I need to identify the last type of military operations, support operations with relation to domestic and/or foreign relief or humanitarian operations. The logistical posture would be operating within a fully mature distribution network. The problem is the event has only disrupted the established sustainment structure the local authorities have had in place. This creates a void in the established structure requiring an external support augmentation to surge sustainment at key locations in order to reestablish continuity creating a static environment (garrison). Because the military part in this type of operation is considered a supporting role to the other domestic or foreign authorities, we have migrated to a different phase, which I will call administrative operations (See Figure 1). This type of operation provides needed support to an area until its own authorities can take over sustainment. The key for this type of operation to be successful is that it lasts only for a short period. If these types of operation extend in time, the community and authorities could start to depend on the augmentation for continuing support rather than their own strength. You will see this when the local governmental infrastructure is immature to start with and then the event has only created additional turmoil.

Types of Military OPNS	Offensive	Defensive	Stability	Support
Structure of Military OPNS	- Movement to Contact - Attack - Exploitation - Pursuit	- Area Defense - Mobile Defense - Retrograded Operations	- Peace OPNS - Foreign Internal Defense - Security Assistance - Humanitarian & Civic Assistance - Support to Insurgences - Combating Terrorism - Noncombatant Evacuation OPNS - Arms Control - Show of Force	- Domestic Support OPNS - Foreign Humanitarian Assistance - Relief OPNS - Support to Incidents Involving WMD - Support to Civil Law Enforcement - Community Assistance
Theater Progression	Immature → Distribution Network → Mature			
Types of Logistical Support OPNS	MANEUVER OPNS	SUSTAINMENT OPNS	MANAGEMENT OPNS	ADMINISTRATIVE OPNS

Figure 1; Logistical Support Operations Sliding Scale

19

Chapter 3

Levels of Logistics

Concept

There are three levels of war discussed in army doctrine. They are strategic, operational and tactical. These levels provide structure to the overall operation. FM 3-0, Operations, states,

1. The Levels of War; "2-3, The Levels of War, The levels of war are doctrinal perspectives that clarify the links between strategic objectives and tactical actions. Although there are no finite limits or boundaries between them, the three levels are strategic, operational and tactical. Understanding the interdependent relationship of all three helps commanders visualize a logical flow of operations, allocate resources, and assign tasks. Actions within the three levels are not associated with a particular command level, unit size, equipment type, or force or component type. Instead, actions are defined as strategic, operational, or tactical based on their effect or contribution to achieving strategic, operational, or tactical objectives".[2]

2. The Strategic Level; "2-4, The strategic level is that level at which a nation, often as one of a group of nations, determines national and multinational security objectives and guidance and develops and uses national resources to accomplish them."[3]

3. The Operational Level; "2-5, The operational level of war is the level at which campaigns and major operations are conducted and sustained to accomplish strategic objectives within theaters or areas of operations (AOs). It links the tactical employment of forces to strategic objectives. The focus at this level is on operational art—the use of military forces to achieve strategic goals through the design, organization, integration, and conduct of theater strategies, campaigns, major operations, and battles. A campaign is a related series of military operations aimed at accomplishing a strategic or operational objective within a given time and space."[4]

---

[2] FM 3-0 (formerly FM 100-5), *Operations*. 14 June 2001, 2-3.

[3] Ibid, 2-4.

[4] Ibid, 2-5.

20

4.   The Tactical Level;

    —   "2-13, tactics is also the realm of close combat, where friendly forces are in immediate contact and use direct and indirect fires to defeat or destroy enemy forces and to seize or retain ground."[5]

    —   "2-14, the operational-level headquarters sets the terms of battle and provides resources for tactical operations. Tactical success is measured by the contribution of an action to the achievement of operationally significant results. Battles and engagements that do not contribute to the campaign objectives, directly or indirectly, are avoided".[6]

The same three levels are also prevalent in logistical operations and the roles they play in support to the combatant commander, FM 4-0, Combat Service Support, states:

1.   Strategic-Level Roles;

    —   "4-6, strategic-level support links the global economic base (people, resources, and industry) to military operations in theater. At this level, the joint staff, military departments, U.S. Transportation Command (USTRANSCOM), Defense Logistics Agency (DLA) , and other DOD agencies focus on force readiness and supporting force projection operations."[7]

    —   "4-7, in force-projection operations, strategic-level support elements fill the distribution pipeline with personnel and materiel resources, and possess the capability to provide services required by the supported joint forces commander (JFC). To support both readiness and force projection, they conduct industrial operations, maintain the industrial base, provide information services, provide strategic-level services (such as depot supply and maintenance, and defense-wide base operations support), and manage strategic stockpiles (such as Army prepositioned assets)."[8]

---

[5] Ibid, 2-13.
[6] Ibid, 2-14
[7] FM 4-0 (FM 100-10), *Combat Service Support,* 29 Aug. 2003, 4-6.
[8] Ibid, 4-7.

2. Operational-Level Roles;

> – "4-47, CSS at the operational level links strategic- and tactical-level CSS. Support personnel at the operational level coordinate support from the strategic level to meet requirements at the tactical level."[9]

> – "4-48, the combatant commander's concept for the campaign or major operation is the basis for support planning. Like strategic-level CSS, operational-level CSS is usually a joint effort and often a multinational effort. Army support at this level is integrated into the total support system required to conduct joint/multinational campaigns and other military activities. The combatant commander's strategic logistics concept will focus on the ability to generate and move forces and materiel in the theater base and to desired operating locations, where operational-level logistics concepts are employed."[10]

> – "4-49, operational-level CSS focuses on theater support operations that involve force generation, force sustainment, and redeployment. The initial focus is on generating a force ready to conduct operations. Sustainment begins during force generation but becomes the primary focus once operations begin."[11]

3. Tactical-Level Roles; "4-66, the goal of CSS at all levels is to generate and sustain combat power at the tactical level. This discussion covers multifunctional organizations and staff functions providing CSS at this level. Detailed discussions of various functional CSS units are in the associated functional chapters of this manual. CSS at the tactical level includes all functions necessary to support battles and engagements. (FM 3-0 and FM 3-90 discuss battles and engagements.) The focus of tactical-level CSS is to provide the CSS necessary to meet the commander's intent and concept of operations, and to maximize his freedom of action. It involves synchronizing all CSS functions. Tactical-level

---

[9] Ibid, 4-47.
[10] Ibid, 4-48.
[11] Ibid, 4-49.

CSS is more immediate than operational-level CSS. Support personnel operate at the forward end of the support pipeline."[12]

As pointed out above the strategic-level roles associate the commercial base to military operations, and provides resources that fills the distribution pipeline. Some functions related to this level of logistical operations are:

- Home Base Support and Services
- Industrial Base
- Strategic Mobility (air & sea)
- Strategic stockpiles and prepositioned resources
- Medical Services and Facilities
- Mobilization and Demobilization

The operational-level roles provide the conduit between the strategic and the tactical levels with sustainment being the primary focus. The logistical support provided consists of force generation, force sustainment, and redeployment. Some functions related to this level of logistical operations are:

- Reception
- Staging
- Onward Movement
- Integration of Forces
- Theater Distribution
- Intra-theater Airlift

The tactical-level role is to generate and sustain combat power as far forward as the foxhole. The main functions conducted at this level are:

- Command and Control
- Distribution-Based System (Factory to the Foxhole, End to End)
  - Arming
  - Manning
  - Fixing
  - Transporting
  - Fueling and their systems

If doctrine is correct and the operational level is the conduit between the tactical and strategic levels with sustainment being the primary focus.

---

[12] Ibid, 4-66.

Then this is where we begin to link the Army centric world of tactical support to Joint Operations where the Army supports its own units, other services, as well as coalition forces under Title X responsibilities for certain commodities and services. The issue is that at the operational level you do not conduct logistics to the tactical level the same way as you do to the strategic level. Yes, you are conducting receive, store, issue, and movement, but under two different battle rhythms.

Theory and Execution

What started me thinking about this was in the summer of 2007 when I was conducting an exercise for the 377 Theater Support Command (TSC). I also had been developing for the Battle Command Sustainment System (BCS3) program manager a cognitive trainer, with support from the Institute for Creative Technologies (ICT) contract managed by the United States (US) Army Research, Development, and Engineering Command (RDECOM) Simulation and Training Technology Center (STTC), teaching distribution management, and how automation can assist. The folks from the Institute for Creative Technologies (ICT) had not spent time in the armed forces so over the past year they have had to learn the distribution management process with no hands-on experiences to taint the process. They were interviewing some colonels from the TSC on the scenarios we were developing for the trainer when the colonels told them that they were all wrong in the way they were conducting logistical support to the scenarios. This confused the ICT personnel and they called me to come over to their location because we had a problem in our scenario development and may have to start all over in creating our scenario. We had been working diligently for the past year interviewing personnel and developing the scenarios so you can understand that I was not fond of the idea to start over. Upon arriving to their location and listening to the problem, the issue then became obvious to me. I had been tasked to develop the cognitive trainer to support the battle rhythm of logistical support from operational to tactical not strategic to operational. To old soldiers that have done these types of operations numerous times in the past it may not be a big deal in switching between the two levels, but for someone who has not been in the military (example contractors), or to young soldiers (officers and non-commission officers) this can be a significant emotional event. In this situation, there really was not any issue. I got the colonels to understand the level of training the game was conducting and the interviews continued without any more problems.

The theory is that at the operational level (example ESC level) the support operations staff is split between two battle rhythms when trying to conduct logistics. This means they have two different reporting and sustainment cycles to deal with. The merging of two different logistical operational battle rhythms means one cycle is supporting operations forward and the other is sustaining operations forward. This is not a new concept and has always been there when conducting logistical support operations, the problem is it has never truly been identified as a staff operational issue, but has always caused problems early in the battle rhythm. Under the tactical level support, you are supporting the battlefield with commodities and services forward as possible to sustain combat operations. This leads to a more compressed time line to complete the reporting and sustainment cycles in support to the operation. When looking back to the strategic level you are projecting existing requirements, forecasting future requirements, and recourses needed to sustain the operational to tactical level support. This change in the operational-tempo can lead to a choke point or cut line between the operational and strategic levels when trying to transfer commodities and movement within the distribution network. This cut line does not only affect the sustainment cycle, but also affects what is to be reported lower to higher between the two levels (tactical and strategic). This difference in time and reported fields can lead to a break in sustainment, or staffs both lower and higher conducting redundant, as well as additional reporting requirements. The following diagram depicts the two different battle rhythms in relationship to the unit staffs and the levels they are operating under (See Figure 2; Levels of Logistical Support Cycle (Commodity Reporting and Movement).

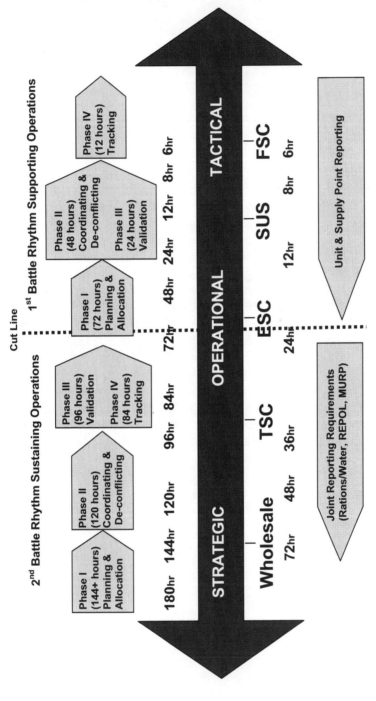

Figure 2; Levels of Logistical Support Cycle (Commodity Reporting and Movement)

As you can see from the above diagram, combat operations dictate the logistical support operational-tempo, so for a staff to calculate the timelines for the reporting and the sustainment cycles, they would simply conduct backward planning from the tactical to the strategic level with the operational level coordinating the different battle rhythms between the two. Therefore, the first and most important battle rhythm is the operational to tactical support consisting of a 24-hour reporting cycle and a 72-hour sustainment cycle in support of the maneuver units. I go in more detail on the purposes and mechanics of the logistical reporting cycle in the section Accounting: Chapter 5, Logistical Reporting and Chapter 7, Reporting and Support Cycle. Once the combatant forces have established combat operations, they begin to expend commodities and resources that need to be replaced within a 12-24 hour period. These projected requirements are identified within a logistical report, which is based on the resupply cycle required to support the operation. In this scenario the theater of support is large enough to constitute a Expeditionary Sustainment Command (ESC) located forward of the Theater Support Command (TSC). In this example, the ESC requires a logistical report every 24-hours where they coordinate two 12-hour sustainment pushes in support of the forward sustainment brigades supporting a region within that 24-hour period. This means that the sustainment brigades are producing a report within a 12-24 hour period supporting a sustainment push every 12 hours. Lastly, the forward support companies are producing a logistical report within an 8-12 hour period supporting sustainment pushes to the brigade combat teams (BCT) utilizing either a one, two, or three push cycle (See figure 3; 1st Battle Rhythm Supporting Operations). This also means the ESC is conducting a 72-hour sustainment cycle forward in support to combat operations. From the ESC to the sustainment brigade (SUS BDE) the sustainment cycle, encompasses a 72-hour planning timeline:

- Phase I (72-hours out) - Planning and Allocation

  − The requirement generated by the logistical report is applied to a Transportation Movement Request (TMR) to the servicing Movement Control Team (MCT) representative either co-located with the Sustainment Brigade (SUS BDE) or located at a regional node.

– The MCT coordinates with regional SUS BDE to fill requirement.

– If the requirement exceeds regional SUS BDE capabilities, the request is passed to the next higher level of command the Movement Control Battalion (MCB) supporting the theater.

– The MCB assesses other SUS BDE's located within the theater for capability to fill the requirement. If one is identified with the proper requirements and capabilities then the MCB transmits the TMR to that servicing MCT for processing and validation.

– The SUS BDE fills requirement or requests assistance from the Theater Sustainment Command.

– The theater MCB can either request support from the SUS BDE supporting that region, task another brigade, or contract capability to satisfy the requirement.

– All associated activities are posted to a distribution matrix for command and control.

- Phase II (48-hours out) Coordinating and De-conflicting

– ESC/MCB/TSC synchronizes requirements for commodities and movement requiring the tasked SUS BDE to begin process of allocating lift assets against the requirement.

– The ESC/MCB/TSC and SUS BDE discuss the mechanics of the movement at a Distribution Movement Board (DMB) meeting where SUS BDE LNO and Theater commodity managers:
  – certify and de-conflict tasking,
  – assign retrograde or backhaul,
  – and coordinate any theater follow-on movements.

– If there is any issue with the customers original request, it can be resubmitted or edited as required.

– The MCT can edit or make any changes to the TMR as necessary.

– If additions or changes are made, the MCB reallocates assets adjusting the existing TMR and submits required changes.

– The SUS BDE submits reports to the ESC/TSC Distribution Management Center (DMC) to confirm movement.

- Phase III (24-hours out) Validation

    – The ESC/MCB/TSC and SUS BDE LNO's conducts DMB either once or twice daily depending on the operational-tempo focusing on next 72-hours.

    – The ESC/MCB/TSC validate the next 24-hour sustainment pushes and tasks the SUS BDE's to assign assets against requirements (crews and load platforms), as well as conduct the following tasks:
    - – task units,
    - – allocate/commit vehicles, and build convoys,
    - – submit Common User Land Transportation (CULT) statues report,
    - – identify Radio Frequency Identification Devises (RFID) tags and Mobile Tracking Systems (MTS), as well as manifests convoys,
    - – identify force protection platforms, their starting point (SP), and time.

    – The MCB validates any retrograde, backhaul, or additional movement with the SUS BDE.

- Phase IV (12-0 hours out) Tracking

    – The MCB/SUS BDE creates operational tracking views of important movement, or their own convoys within the Battle Command Sustainment Support System (BCS3).

    – The regional MCT report positive inbound clearance (PIC) of movement within their area of responsibility (starting and closing reports)

– The MCB/MCT/SUS BDE can create a proximity report capability within BCS3 to and share information to assist in convoy tracking, and PIC closure reports.

– The MCB/MCT/SUS BDE's confirm any retrograde, backhaul, or additional movement.

The diagram below shows a closer look at the first battle rhythm and the reporting and sustainment functions required in the prescribed period (See figure 3; 1st Battle Rhythm Supporting Operations).

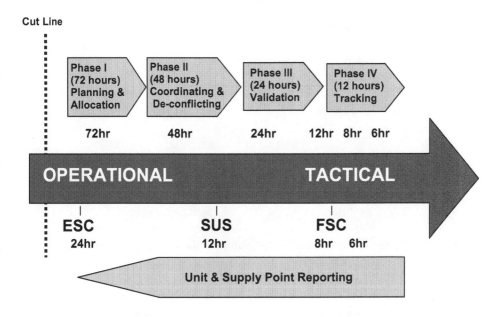

Figure 3; 1st Battle Rhythm Supporting Operations

The second battle rhythm is sustaining operations and it consists of the operational to strategic level support made up of a 48-72 hour reporting cycle and a 144+-hour sustainment cycle in support of sustaining the combat operations forward. The ESC then is producing a logistical report with a joint flavor (example are Rations/Water, Reporting Emergency Petroleum, Oils, And Lubricants (REPOL), and Munitions Report (MURP) all joint level US DoD report formats) to the TSC within a 24-36 hour period. The TSC produces a logistical requirement report to either the Department of the Army, Defense Logistics Agency (DLA), Army Material Command (AMC), Host Nation, or contract agencies within a 48-72+ hour period. This function of requesting requirements has been backward planned so commodities and resources arrive in theater within an proper timeline so they can receive and coordinate onward movement to sustain combat operations forward (See figure 4; 2nd Battle Rhythm Sustaining Operations). This also means the TSC is conducting a 144+-hour sustainment cycle forward to sustain combat operations. From the time, commodities and resources arrive in theater and until the TSC can coordinate onward movement to the ESC it could very easily encompasses a 144+-hour planning timeline:

- Phase I (144+-hours out) - Planning and Allocation

    – The requirement generated by the logistical report applied to a Transportation Movement Request (TMR) to the servicing Movement Control Team (MCT) representative either co-located with the Sustainment Brigade (SUS BDE) or located at a regional node.

    – The MCT coordinates with regional SUS BDE to fill requirement.

    – If the requirement exceeds regional SUS BDE capabilities, the request is passed to the next higher level of command the Movement Control Battalion (MCB) supporting the theater.

    – The MCB assesses other capabilities within theater (task another brigade, host nation or contracted support) to fill the requirement. If one is identified with the proper requirements and capabilities then the MCB transmits the TMR to that servicing MCT for processing and validation.

    – The SUS BDE fills requirement or requests assistance from the Theater Sustainment Command for additional or augmented support or assets from another brigade, host nation, or contracted elements.

– The theater MCB can either request support from the SUS BDE supporting that region, task another brigade, or contract capability to satisfy requirement.

– All associated activities are posted to a distribution matrix for command and control.

- Phase II (120-hours out) Coordinating and De-conflicting

– TSC/MCB synchronizes requirements for commodities and movement requiring the tasked SUS BDE to begin process of allocating lift assets against the requirement.

– The TSC/MCB/ESC and SUS BDE discuss the mechanics of the movement at a Distribution Movement Board (DMB) meeting where ESC and SUS BDE LNO's, and Theater commodity managers:
    – certify and de-conflict tasking,
    – assign retrograde or backhaul,
    – coordinate any theater follow-on movements.

– If there is any issue with the customers original request, it can be resubmitted or edited as required.

– The MCT can edit or make any changes to the TMR as necessary.

– If additions or changes are made the MCB reallocates assets adjusting the existing TMR and submits required changes.

– The SUS BDE submits reports to the TSC Distribution Management Center (DMC) to confirm movement.

- Phase III (96-hours out) Validation

– The TSC/MCB and ESC/SUS BDE LNO's conduct DMB either once or twice daily depending on the operational-tempo focusing on next 144+-hours.

– The TSC/MCB validate the next 96-hour sustainment pushes and task the SUS BDE's to assign assets against

requirements (crews and load platforms), as well as conducts the following tasks:
  – task units,
  – allocate/commit vehicles, and build convoys,
  – submit Common User Land Transportation (CULT) statues report,
  – identify Radio Frequency Identification Devises (RFID) tags and Mobile Tracking Systems (MTS), as well as manifests convoys,
  – identify force protection platforms, their starting point (SP), and time.

– The MCB validates any retrograde, backhaul, or additional movement with the SUS BDE.

▪ Phase IV (84-0 hours out) Tracking

  – The MCB/SUS BDE creates operational tracking views of important movement, or their own convoys within the Battle Command Sustainment Support System (BCS3).

  – The regional MCT reports positive inbound clearance (PIC) of movement within their area of responsibility (starting and closing reports)

  – The MCB/MCT/SUS BDE can create a proximity report capability within BCS3 to and share information to assist in convoy tracking, and PIC closure reports.

  – The MCB/MCT/SUS BDE's confirms any retrograde, backhaul, or additional movement.

The diagram below shows a closer look at the second battle rhythm and the reporting and sustainment functions required in the proscribed period (See figure 4; 2nd Battle Rhythm Sustaining Operations).

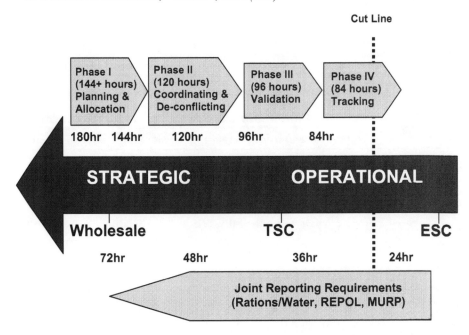

Figure 4; 2nd Battle Rhythm Sustaining Operations

As stated above, doctrine says that the operational level is the conduit between the tactical and strategic levels with sustainment being the primary focus. To understand the mechanics and functions of end-to-end distribution management you must recognize the different staff procedures and timelines required at the operational level before you will be able to execute the proper battle rhythm required for supporting and sustaining combat operations forward.

Chapter 4

Distribution Networks

Concept

For the last five years, the Army has been moving forward to integrate the Distribution Management (DM) Process and Army Transformation into the new logistical structure of the future with some successes. The real concern is that it is not realistic to operate both concepts in their pure conceptual form. Under the Distribution Management Process, units would live off the flow and there would be no need for intermediate stocks forward and for transformation, there would be only one battle set or force structure required to meet all situations. The issue is the distribution network that the logistician is required to operate within can be as much of an enemy as the human one we are there to fight. The limitations in the network's physical construction and our resources that we bring to the fight can hamper our ability to conquer time, distance, and space requirements in support of maneuver forces. Both concepts need the flexibility to adapt to the environment they are going to operate within, thus allowing the military to create hybrid versions of both concepts while still providing operational procedures and structures to meet the needs of the distribution network and offer the proper battle setting. Logistical planners must have the vision to enhance the network with additional capabilities and tailor assets to meet shortfalls in reference to physical or resources required. The Distribution Management Process is based on visibility of information to maximize capacity of systems and to control the pipeline. Transformation is based on creating a force structure that is modular in composition and can be tailored by components to meet the situation. FM 3-0, Operations, Chapter 12-50,
Combat Service Support Factors Influencing Operational
Reach and Sustainability, states;

> "The Army logistical system in theater operates within the joint theater distribution system (see JP 4-01.4; FM 4-01.4). The distribution system consists of several interrelated networks: communications and automation, physical, and resource. These networks provide the asset visibility necessary for efficient and effective distribution. The communications and automation network distributes and correlates CSS data across the force, while assisting all commanders with management of the information. The

physical network consists of the quantity and capability of fixed structures and established facilities.

It includes factories, warehouses, airfields, seaports, roads, railroads, inland waterways, pipelines, terminals, bridges, tunnels, and buildings. These facilities can be located in CONUS, at an ISB, at a forward deployed base, or in theater. The resource network consists of the people, materiel, and machines operating within and over the physical network." [13]

Theory and Execution

With all this said, it is apparent that the distribution network is the logistician's battle space. Focusing on its construction, control and even its manipulation, is a definite requirement for the success in supporting maneuver forces on today's modern battlefield. Normally, offensive operations are conducted in a linear operational environment and within a contiguous area of operations, which supports an undeveloped distribution network. As the conflict moves toward stability and sustainment operations, so must the distribution network progress to a nonlinear operational set, within either a contiguous or noncontiguous area of operations (AO). Nonlinear operations generally center on multiple decisive points, which correlate to the logistical lines of communication (LOC) existing between operating bases within the distribution network. These lines of communication, or convoy routes that resupply, are dependent on the ability to protect the element throughout its travel. However, when the freedom of movement in the lines of communications is threatened, linear operations should be considered. The problem exists that when operating within a nonlinear operational set then every line of communication of the linear battlefields within the nonlinear construct requires route clearance and convoy security, between specific boundaries and a number of passage of lines among different maneuver units and designated area of operations. Operations like these add much to the confusion and congestion of the maneuver commander's battle space, and take away maneuver forces to support convoy security operations. To remove the strain of these types of operations, combat service support units will synchronize subordinate unit actions in time, distance and space with the intent to link convoy operations with tactical execution. To explain this synchronization, it is best if the logistician establishes a battle rhythm

---

[13] FM 3-0 (formerly FM 100-5), *Operations*. 14 June 2001, 12-17.

between the daily distribution pushes and the contingency stock levels based on the customer's daily consumption rate and the delivery time, distance and space that are required to get supplies to meet Time Definite Delivery (TDD) requirements. Due to time, distance, and space constraints it may not be feasible to deliver all commodities each and everyday. For example, the time and distance it takes one convoy to re-supply a customer may take two days in duration to convoy, making the re-supply cycle every three days. The space issue is different in that because of the enemy's actions or other events, it could make the environment either difficult or at times the re-supply on the set cycle will not occur. For example - the enemy blocks or damages the lines of communications, or because of events such as political, religious, weather, or tactical missions it could create the circumstances that temporarily or even for a number of days, deprive re-supply of commodities to the consumer. This requires the need for additional commodities to be located at strategic hubs and forward logistic nodes, thus providing for continued re-supply until that time the standards re-supply cycle can be resumed. These stocks are contingency stock to be utilized during re-supply delays and surge operations. Daily consumption rates are forecasted and reported higher to adjust commodity re-supply rates to compensate for missed rotation cycles to maintain the proper additional days of supply needed forward for contingency stocks, as well as required daily consumption stock. Remember, if the customer lives off the flow and the flow equals the consumption rates, then any additional stocks forward are for area support, contingency usage or required rotation cycle of stocks. In support of this synchronization, the logistician produces a sustainment cycle, which is visible at all levels to provide situational awareness and synergy for planning and coordination between logistical and maneuver staff elements. These scheduled re-supply operations are based on beginning consumption rates and should be adjusted from reported data. Doctrine states that in supporting combat operations, the logistician pushes supplies forward with or without the requirement for consist reporting cycle. As long as the lines of communications are open and whenever the beginning support cycle is established, it is then pushed regardless of any reporting from the unit, or until the unit submits a report to adjust the cycle. Once offensive operations are over, then an operational pause occurs and the battlefield requirement moves to a sustainment mode of support. A standard reporting and sustainment cycle is then submitted and items are sent by priority and importance to the unit. In the following chapters, I will provide an in-depth description of reporting and support cycles.

LTC James H. Henderson, "Cotton", USA (Ret.)

For both concepts to work, a distribution network has to be established from the beginning of combat operations to support an immature infrastructure, as well as to evolve over time to support the expectations of the projected mature infrastructure for future campaigns. Under the new logistical force structure, the Theater establishes and controls the Main Supply Routes (MSR) and the Brigade Combat Teams (BCT) or divisional structure establish and control Alternate Supply Routes (ASR). The combination of both types of routes, the incorporation of alternate modes of transportation (air, rail, and sea), the placement of in-transit visibility (ITV) devices throughout the network consisting of Radio Frequency Identification (RFID) tags, vehicle tracking devices, fixed and hand-held interrogators capable of tracking the flow of commodities and movement, the positioning of Logistical Support Areas (LSA), Forward Staging Bases (FOB), Intermediate Support Bases (ISB), Supply Support Activities (SSA), Trailer Transfer Points (TTP), Rest Over Night Sites (RON), and Movement Control Teams (MCT), Highway Regulation Teams (HRT), Cargo Documentation Teams, Distribution Management Teams (DMT), and other Supply personnel for data collecting, locating, tracking, and reporting - are being integrated to provide the configuration of the distribution network. The management of the Distribution Network is the key to logistical flow and the implementation of the Distribution Management Process. The Distribution Management Process establishes a battle rhythm for movement control centered on a Common Operating Picture (COP) between sustainment, movement and force protection, linking the three with In-Transit Visibility (ITV) assets to improve force tracking and support distribution and ultimately providing synergy at all levels.

Accounting

Chapter 5

Logistical Reporting

Concept

The logistical (LOG) report is a logistics status report from a unit to its higher headquarters, which provides a current logistical picture that identifies requirements, projections, and forecasts that gives visibility on critical shortages, readiness, and offers input to the common operating picture (COP). It is most commonly a manual report conducted from lower to higher providing information on commodities and services that does not have a Standard Army Management Information Systems (STAMIS) capability to identify sustainment requirements.

The LOG Report is utilized to program and confirm allocation of supplies to maintain a unit at authorized levels. The report allows the higher command and supporting units to analyze the situation and make assessments on allocation, priority, and synchronization in order to sustain the force. The report is not to be used to report the same information available within the STAMIS, or as a way to requisition supplies managed by a STAMIS. The only time this is not the case is when most commonly STAMIS is not operational because a unit is on the move. Additional reports such as the Maintenance Readiness Report (MRR), Munitions Report (MUREP) and Petroleum Report (REPOL) should not be added to reporting requirements for subordinate units below division-level when STAMIS and LOG Reporting information satisfy information requirements.

Theory and Execution

After in-depth thought and many conversations on the topic, I have concluded, "*that not all levels of command forecast, some levels only report*", and that when a level forecasts it is because their requirements have exceeded their own resourced capabilities and require additional assistance. The key point here relates to the old saying, "words mean everything and everything means words".

You should never get the terms **requirement**, **projection**, and **forecast** mixed up or you could easily request too much of a commodity, which then creates excess and ties up resources. So let us discuss the differences between these three terms. A requirement is what a unit needs to sustain itself for a 24-hour period. Projection is based on the hauling/storage capacity of a unit applied against the requirement and the number of times a unit can be resupplied within a 24-hour period. If a unit's requirement exceeds its capability to be resupplied within 24-hours then the unit has identified a shortfall with its projection. Last, a forecast is required when the requirement exceeds its projected capability identifying a shortfall, and additional resources are required to fulfill the initial requirement. This normally continues throughout the sustainment cycle until that time the requirement is no longer needed, or the unit is cross-leveled or augmented by additional capabilities.

To explain the theory in some detail, a maneuver company, battalion, and the sustainment battalion levels of command strictly has a requirement; they need so much of a commodity a day to maintain operations, so bottom line they report the requirement. There is no forecasting, only reporting a requirement and its time projection. An example of this would be if their daily requirement for fuel is 150,000 gallons a day and their storage and hauling capacity is 50,000 gallons a day, their LOG Report will reflect a daily requirement of 150,000 gallons and projection of three pushes of 50,000 gallons in a 24-hour period. Anymore than three pushes in a 24-hour period exceeds their supported capability. However, let us take it further. What if the units are moving 100 kilometers a day and this increases their fuel requirement to 200,000 gallons a day and their storage and hauling capacity is 50,000 gallons a day? Their LOG Report will reflect a daily requirement of 200,000 gallons and projection of three pushes of 50,000 gallons in a 24-hour period showing a shortfall of 50,000 gallons of fuel to support the movement. Upon receiving the LOG Report the S4 of the Brigade Combat Team (BCT) identifies the shortfall of 50,000 gallons of fuel to support the movement and on his/her LOG Report forecasts for the additional requirement of 50,000 gallons and resources to support the operation. Bottom line if you did not report the discrepancy between the requirement and the projection to identify the shortfall, then the underlining requirement of additional assistance and resources may not have been seen to be forecasted. To solve this situation always have the units report within their hauling/storage capacities. By doing this you identify shortfalls in resources and time, so higher can always see when they are required to forecast.

Under the new modular force concept, there are two options in the ways logistical reporting and tasking can be conducted. Options one, have the maneuver and the sustainment (BSB) battalions reporting requirements to the higher brigade combat team (BCT), allowing the maneuver battalion to direct task the forward support company (FSC). Units can report up to battalion level using either manual or automated systems like Battle Command Sustainment Support System (BCS3) or Force XXI Battle Command Brigade and Below (FBCB2) when possible. Depending upon command and control relationships, the forward support company may provide internal logistical reporting to the sustainment battalion or the supported unit. In any case, the supported unit's logistical report is coordinated with the sustainment battalion. Each level of command from the Company to the Corps can direct tasking to its subordinate units of logistical assets for the purpose of mission accomplishment. I myself have problems with this option because it takes the sustainment battalion commander and staff out of the picture to assist in planning and coordination between the maneuver battalion and the forward support company, which hinders additional coordination with theater support (See Figure 5; Option 1 - lower to higher Logistical Reporting Flow). By the maneuver battalion, staff having direct tasking over the forward support company you have removed the senior logistician from assisting the forward support company commander, most times a captain level with no more than four to eight years experience. You have also stifled the sustainment battalion logistical staff element that could directly assist in the synchronization of logistical operation between the maneuver element and the forward support company, as well as the theater support.

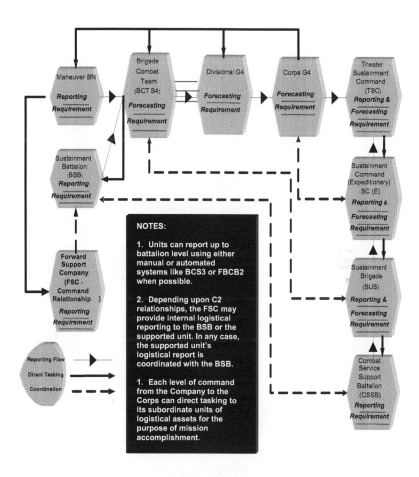

NOTES:

1. Units can report up to battalion level using either manual or automated systems like BCS3 or FBCB2 when possible.

2. Depending upon C2 relationships, the FSC may provide internal logistical reporting to the BSB or the supported unit. In any case, the supported unit's logistical report is coordinated with the BSB.

1. Each level of command from the Company to the Corps can direct tasking to its subordinate units of logistical assets for the purpose of mission accomplishment.

Figure 5; Option 1 - lower to higher Logistical Reporting Flow

Now option two, in my opinion, provides a better solution to the equation. Option two has the maneuver and the brigade sustainment battalions (BSB) reporting requirements to the higher brigade combat team (BCT) as option one, but does not allow the maneuver battalion to direct task the forward support company (FSC). It has the brigade combat team providing direct tasking to the sustainment battalion and then to the forward support company. It also allows for the forward support company and the sustainment battalion to conduct coordination with the maneuver battalion to improve synchronization of the logistical reporting process (See Figure 6; Option 2 - lower to higher Logistical Reporting Flow). As above, it allows units to report up to battalion level using either manual or automated systems like Battle Command Sustainment Support System (BCS3) or Force XXI Battle Command Brigade and Below (FBCB2) when possible. Moreover, it spells out the relationship between each level of command for direct tasking to its subordinate units of logistical assets for the purpose of mission accomplishment. This option provides for the influence and involvement of the sustainment battalion commander and staff to assist in planning and coordination between the maneuver battalion and the forward support company, as well as conduct coordination with theater support units. In my opinion, this option provides for a cleaner task organization making better sense, and displaces an easier change of command that subordinates can understand.

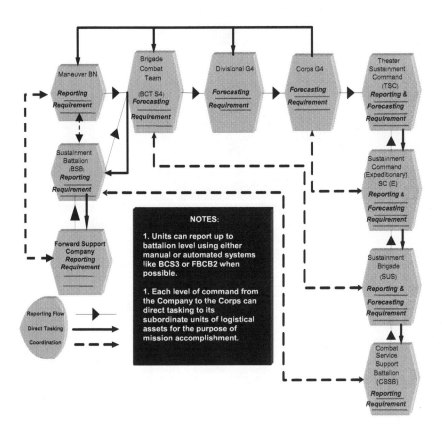

Figure 6; Option 2 - lower to higher Logistical Reporting Flow

Logistical Reporting Flow

Let us review the logistical (LOG) Reporting flow by the different command levels tasks to see how the process should work. The key terms are as follows:

1. **Requirement** is what a unit needs to sustain itself for a 24-hour period.

2. **Projection** is based on the hauling/storage capacity of a unit applied against the requirement, and the number of times a unit can be resupplied within a 24-hour period.

3. **Forecast** is required when the requirement exceeds its projected capability identifying a shortfall, and additional resources are required to fulfill the initial requirement.

The key point to remember when conducting LOG reporting is it always starts at the lowest level and goes up, and that should make perfect sense because the requirements start at the company and battalion levels. Therefore, we will begin with the maneuver battalion-reporting phase. At this phase of reporting, the companies and the battalion only have requirements and projections, so that is all that will be reported to the brigade combat team S4. The companies submit their report; the S4 adds any internal requirements and rolls the two up into one report. Upon completion of roll-up, the report is validated and sent to the brigade combat team S4 (See Figure 7; Maneuver Battalion Reporting Flow).

Figure 7; Maneuver Battalion Reporting Flow

The next phase is the brigade combat team reporting, which starts with the different maneuver and sustainment (BSB) battalions submitting their LOG report to the brigade combat team S4. This is the first level that can provide not only requirements and projections, but also can add forecasted requirements. The brigade S4 takes the battalion requirements and reviews the projections to determine if any forecasting requirements exist. If so, the brigade S4 takes the battalion requirements and the forecasted requirements and rolls the two up into one report. Once complete the report is validated and sent to the division S4, and the brigade S4 conducts coordination with the supporting sustainment brigade, and provides direct tasking to their brigade sustainment battalions (BSB) who then can start to coordinate with the supported maneuver battle and supporting combat service support battalion (See Figure 8; Brigade Combat Team Reporting Flow).

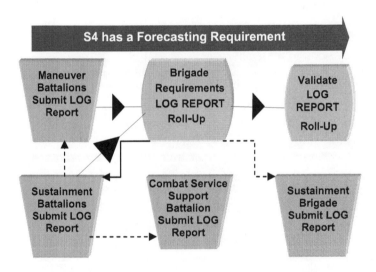

Figure 8; Brigade Combat Team Reporting Flow

The next phase in this process is the division reporting phase where the different brigade combat teams submit their requirements, projections, and forecasting to their division G4. This level can provide requirements, projections, forecasting. The division G4 takes the brigades requirements and reviews the projections to determine if any forecasting requirements exist. If so, the division G4 takes the brigades requirements and the forecasted requirements and rolls the two up into one report. Once complete the report is validated and sent to the corps G4, and the division G4 conducts coordination with the supporting expeditionary sustainment command, and the brigades conduct coordination with their supporting sustainment brigade (See Figure 9; Division Reporting Flow).

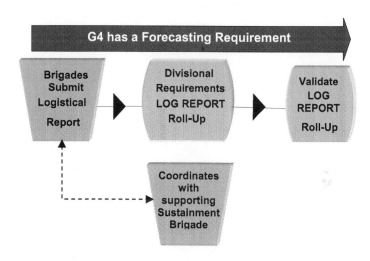

Figure 9; Division Reporting Flow

The corps reporting phase is next where the divisions submit their requirements, projections, and forecasting to the corps G4. This level can provide requirements, projections, and forecasting. The corps G4 takes the division's requirements and reviews the projections and forecasting requirements. Then the corps G4 takes the division's requirements and the forecasted requirements and rolls the two up into one report. Once complete the report is validated and sent to the theater support command (TSC), and the corps G4 and divisions G4 conducts coordination with the supporting expeditionary sustainment command (See Figure10; Corps Reporting Flow).

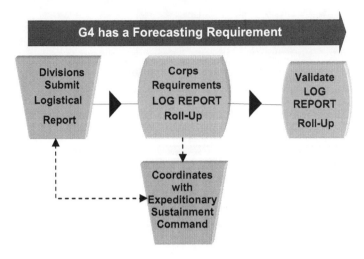

Figure 10; Corps Reporting Flow

The next phase is the theater sustainment command-reporting phases were the corps submits their requirements, projections, and forecasting to the theater sustainment command, but also the theater subordinate unit the expeditionary sustainment command submits their lower to higher consolidated report. At this level only the support operations officer (SPO) can conduct forecasting. The theater sustainment command G4 provides the internal support required for the organization and submits the parent unit's requirements and projections to the SPO for incorporation into an overall theater sustainment command report. Remember the theater G4 does not forecast. The theaters SPO reviews the external support requirements and forecasting from the corps G4, the expeditionary sustainment command and any area support requirements, includes the internal requirements from the theater G4, and rolls them up into one report. Once complete the report is validated and sent to higher (See Figure 11; Theater Sustainment Command (TSC) Reporting Flow).

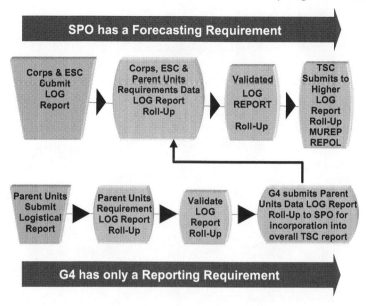

Figure 11; Theater Sustainment
Command (TSC) Reporting Flow

Now the sustainment support units begin their lower to higher reporting flow and we start with the expeditionary sustainment command (ESC). The corps, divisions, and sustainment brigades submit their requirements, projections, and forecasting to the expeditionary sustainment command. Also at this level only the support operations officer (SPO) can conduct forecasting. The expeditionary sustainment command G4 provides the internal support required for the organization and submits the parent unit's requirements and projections to the SPO for incorporation into an overall report. Remember the expeditionary sustainment command G4 does not forecast. The expeditionary sustainment command SPO reviews the external support requirements and forecasting from the corps, divisions, and sustainment brigades, additional area support requirements, includes the internal requirements from the expeditionary sustainment command G4, and rolls them up into one report. Once complete the report is validated and sent to higher. The expeditionary sustainment command SPO also has a requirement to submit additional reports to the theater sustainment command consisting of a Munitions Report (MUREP) and a Petroleum Report (REPOL). These reports are complied from data received from supported and subordinate units' reports (See Figure12; Expeditionary Sustainment Command (ESC) Reporting Flow).

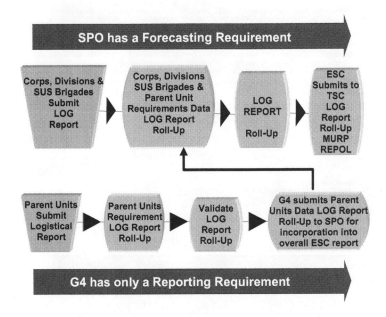

**Figure 12; Expeditionary Sustainment
Command (ESC) Reporting Flow**

Next are the sustainment brigades reporting phase. The brigade combat teams submit their requirements, projections, and forecasting to their supporting sustainment brigade. Also at this level only the support operations officer (SPO) can conduct forecasting. The sustainment brigade S4 provides the internal support required for the organization and submits the parent unit's requirements and projections to the SPO for incorporation into an overall report. Remember the sustainment brigade S4 does not forecast. The sustainment brigade SPO reviews the external support requirements and forecasting from the brigade combat teams and area support requirements, includes the internal requirements from the sustainment brigade S4, and rolls them up into one report. Once complete the report is validated, and it is sent to expeditionary sustainment command. (See Figure 13; Sustainment Brigade Reporting Flow).

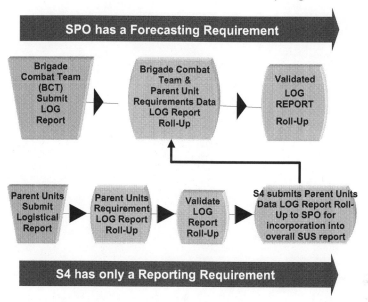

Figure 13; Sustainment Brigade Reporting Flow

Last is the combat service support battalions reporting phase. The sustainment battalions submit their requirements and projections to their supporting battalion. Also at this level only the support operations officer (SPO) can conduct forecasting. The battalion S4 provides the internal support required for the organization and submits the parent unit's requirements and projections to the SPO for incorporation into an overall report, remember the battalion S4 does not forecast. The combat service support battalions SPO reviews the external support requirements and forecasting from the sustainment battalions, includes the internal requirements from the combat service support battalions S4, and rolls them up into one report. Once complete the report is validated, and sends to the sustainment brigade. (See Figure 14; Combat Service Support Battalion (CSSB) Reporting Flow).

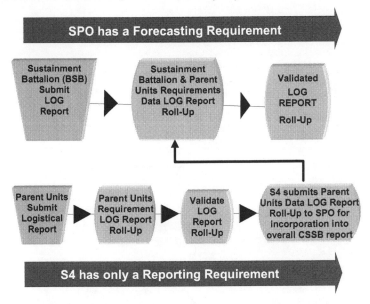

Figure 14; Combat Service Support Battalion (CSSB) Reporting Flow

Chapter 6

Battlefield Accounting – Forecasting vs. STAMIS

Concept

The model is centered around the idea that you conduct supply operations during wartime by focusing on forecasted manual reports, lower to higher, rolled up at the divisional, corps, and theater levels, and managing with the Standard Army Management Information Systems (STAMIS). You support garrison supply operations by focusing on STAMIS data, and managing with forecasted information.

Theory and Execution

In support of this concept, let us review the process of ordering the four major classes of supply required to support wartime operations class I (water and rations), class III (bulk fuel), class V (ammunition), and critical class IX (critical repair parts to maintain combat power). First, at the corps and theater level, the unit during war is not required to process a material release order (MRO) into the Standard Army Retail Supply System (SARSS) to receive water, rations or critical repair parts. Those higher-level support management elements assess the units forecast, then review the STAMIS data to identify the commodities by type, quantities and location, and then direct the sustainment brigade to issue the supplies to the unit forecasting the requirement and apply for the transportation movement request (TMR) to ship the commodity to the units area supply support activity. Second, there is not a STAMIS that is used to account for class III bulk fuels (JP8, DF2, or MOGAS), so it is requested and processed the same as water and rations. Third, though ammunition has a STAMIS, it is only utilized at the local Ammunition Supply Points (ASP), as the computer system does not conduct a theater roll-up of all ASPs providing stock levels. Ammunition at the corps and theater levels is managed off manual spreadsheets providing a theater roll-up by type and is processed the same as class I and III bulk fuel. Fourth, SARSS-1 issues by date time group and priority, and there is not a viable supply referral system in a wartime environment. SARSS-1 issues by oldest and lowest priority on the requisition, but in wartime, everybody uses priority one and the priority on the requisition may not match the commanders changing unit priority used to conduct the battle. For the process to work the theater manager has to contact the supply activity and direct the priority of issue by operational priority and have the requests processed by those requirements, not by the SARSS-1 business rules. To add to the priority problem within SARSS due to the lack of freedom of movement on the battlefield, the SARSS-1 capability to conduct referrals automatically between supply support activities is not an option within the battle space. This is because there isn't a standard delivery network established between supply nodes, due either to lack of assets, enemy operations or route restrictions prohibiting standard supply runs as conducted on a garrison or installation type environment (sometimes called FedEx runs). Last and most important, wartime supply is time-sensitive and may not have the timeframe to process the request through the business rules established within SARSS-1. The SARSS-1 automation cycle of processing requisitions may not match the sustainment cycle required to aid the needs of the battle. This point alone makes it impractical to conduct supply sustainment during war strictly by STAMIS and not by forecasting.

In a garrison environment, it is just the opposite.
Supply managers utilize STAMIS to run the daily operations and manage forecasting to depict supply surges or declining requirements. In garrison Class I and IX, supply activities adhere to the SARSS-1 business rules of issuing commodities. Most requests are not time sensitive and there are the proper timeframes to let the automated cycle process work, but most importantly, there is a workable referral system in garrison or between installation locations, facilitating SARSS-1 automatically processing referrals between other supply activities and a standard delivery network is established among supply nodes. Yes, there is FedEx capability. For class III (bulk fuel) and class V (ammunition), the unit goes to their local supply point and orders the commodities in a timely manner to insure the activity has the proper amount of required forecasted dates the unit needs. Again, time is not a factor - the unit has the time to plan and prepare for the operation.

Chapter 7

Reporting and Support Cycle

Concept

Reporting by definition is segments of information describing certain elements, or an account of certain events given or presented to someone. A cycle is a gap of space or time in which one set of events is completed. This process completes one rotation and then repeats in the same sequence. In the distribution management process, these functions are required to provide information lower to higher (reporting), and to depict a sustainment battle rhythm the support operations officer (SPO) utilizes to sustain the units conducting the operation (support or sustainment cycle). They are separate procedures nested with the battle rhythm in support of one another. The report is also on a cycle to provide the most timely and relevant information possible, and the support cycle is based off the information provided by the report, and the priority and timeline of the units to be sustained. The key for the battle rhythm to be relevant in support of the operation the staff must understand the information provided by the report and the actions occurring within the support cycle could be on different gaps of time creating a picture of real or near real-time information. This is not a problem as long as the staff understands which rotation of the sustainment cycle they are conducting, and how old the data is in relation to the events occurring. An example you are on the first 12-hour push of the third day sustainment rotation, and the reported data is 6-hours old utilizing a 12-hour reporting cycle when the first support cycle push begins. The problem exists when the staffs mixes information from different reporting periods.

Theory and Execution

It must be pointed out that the capability to populate real or near real-time data is a great achievement and is the bases for the Distribution Management process to work properly. The staff managing the process has to know what reporting and support cycle they are operating under, so the real time data does not keep changing the current reporting and support cycle. Mixing real-time data with the support cycle can create a perception with the commander that the support plan does not assist the customer. Real time data is only good for the time-period the logistician can affect.

An example is the unit on a 6-hour reporting cycle. Given a 6-hour reporting cycle, the commodities requested from that report are 12-hours out from being delivered to the customer. For an 8-hour reporting cycle, delivery would be 16-hours out and on a 12-hour reporting cycle, delivery would be 24 hours out. This does not mean the real time data cannot identify emergency requirements that could affect earlier reaction within the cycle (a portion of the support could be sent earlier than 12, 16 or 24 hours). For the real-time data to be relevant, the logistician has to be able to act on it during the current cycle. If the logistician cannot react in the current cycle, he then plans for the next cycle. The real-time data that might confuse the commanding general is during the morning or nightly Battle Update Assessment (BUA). The logistics staff is briefing the combat fleet slide by current reporting and support cycle, but the maneuver brigade commander briefs his combat readiness as of fifteen minutes prior to the briefing with a lower readiness percentage than the general's staff . The commanding general becomes concerned that his staff is not supporting the maneuver commanders' needs due to the difference in readiness numbers. The briefer is unable to convince the commanding general that the current sustainment cycle, which is either moving or preparing to deliver, is sufficient to meet the current identified deadline vehicles and they will use the new updated figures in the calculations for the next sustainment cycle. Bottom line, there is no emergency. The maneuver commander's staff is reporting a different cycle. The commanding general's staff needs to synchronize the reporting cycle and, if necessary, have portions of the report updated and submitted more than once per cycle. An example of this is having the combat readiness by fleet updated and submitted once on its regular cycle time, and two other times one hour prior to the morning and evening Battle Update Assessment (BUA). This provides a true snapshot in time of the combat readiness of the fleets giving the commander a near real time view for planning and decision-making.

The maneuver brigade commander report is merely a

Slant Report that gives a snapshot of what equipment needs to be validated within the supply system under the next support cycle (See Figure 15; Reporting Cycle).

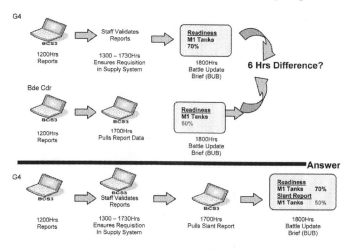

Figure 15; Reporting Cycle

To meet operational consideration, the data received from the Standard Army Maintenance System (SAMS-1 or 2) and displayed within the Battle Command Sustainment System (BCS3) is viewed as a Slant Report, until ILAP has received the gateway information and publishes its data to the network updating the SAMS data, producing a validated report. The key is synchronization of the data exchange so all staff levels change to the updated data at the same time. A good Common Operating Picture (COP) is the battle rhythm between sustainment and movement applying data for utilization at all levels and providing synergy.

Chapter 8

Capacity Management

Concept

The Capacity Management provides for efficient use of resources to achieve an optimal level of performance. An effective transport and logistics process helps to ensure that resources are used in the best place, at the right time, and in the correct quantity to support logistical operations, and is a key ingredient in successfully conducting the Distribution Management Process.

Capacity management is a multi-faceted methodology that includes planning, analyzing, sizing, optimizing, and managing information associated with transportation resource capacity. The process encompasses several iterative functions:

1. Analyzing cargo and transport equipment

2. Modeling various transport options

3. Optimizing a cargo movement plan

4. Monitoring the actual movement of convoys

5. Modifying and tuning a convoy plan

The method involves both procedures and systems and it includes multiple facets of business service planning and management to include specification, implementation, monitoring, analysis, and tuning of the final plan.
An effective capacity management method helps users to respond quickly and effectively to logistical operational needs. This, in turn, makes it possible to add resources in time to prevent the adverse impact associated with a shortfall of equipment or supplies in a support operation.

Theory and Execution

To understand the mechanics of capacity management we need to review the functionality that is currently in place and the new functionality and ideas in developing a functional manual or automated Capacity Management Tool. The method and procedures for a workable system are based on the following objectives:

1. Manage the development of polices dealing with commodity and movement requirements.

2. Alert the user to violations of transportation and logistics policy.

3. Create movement plans using data entered by transportation and commodity planners, imported from other logistical sources and related logistics reporting systems.

4. Add the capability to existing automated applications to ensure an easy interface with related systems such as the Army's Battle Command Sustainment Support System (BCS3) and the Transportation Coordinators-Automated Information for Movements System II (TC-AIMS II).

This chapter also provides a foundation for defining the business and functional requirements need in developing a Capacity Management process, and can serve as a basis for thought in creating doctrinal procedures in conducting capacity management.

Business Requirements

To create a workable methodology we must identify the business procedures and guidelines that the tool must achieve. These business rules are the platform for the tools functions and capabilities. You need to first develop a comprehensive list of business requirements that are the basis for the system to police capacity management tools purpose and ability. The following are some ideas of certain procedures and guidelines that need to be included:

- The method requires a need to generate a running estimate of transport vehicle capacity and convoy capacity, and data will be filtered according to user defined policies and requirements.

- The method requires alerting the user to policy violations.

- The method requires generating movement plans for the user.

- Moreover, if making the tool an automated application, the method requires a need to have the capability to exist on a software and application independent platform.

In sum, the Capacity Management methodology will facilitate transportation and logistics resource planning, allocation, and implementation (Table 1; Business Requirements).

Table 1: Business Requirements

Feature	Description
Adherence to Set Rules and Policies	The method requires acceptance of user parameter input of set rules for the operation or relating to military logistical operations in the theater. This input will vary by location, mission, or operation. Input includes data associated with the number of vehicles per convoy, special Host Nation (HN) escort requirements, military to commercial ratios, number of containerization and consolidation locations, and Convoy Protection Platform (CPP) to truck ratios. Method of processing requires the system to adhere to the following parameters example: - No more than 30 platforms to include gun trucks - Minimum platforms = 5 - Maximum platforms = 28 - Minimum CCP 2, Maximum CCP 4

	▪ On commercial (or white) truck convoys every 5th platform is a military (or green) truck ▪ Route Black-Out Times ▪ Security Movement Window The method needs to accommodate requirements and policies that change periodically and that differ among areas of operations (AO). The theater manager should have the ability to modify requirements in theater.
Monitoring	During the planning and allocation phases, the system will apply these rules and alert the user to any violations of these rules. The method needs to generate alerts on rules set for Convoy Protection Platforms (CPP) depending on theater, destination, and route. If the proper number of assets is unavailable and requirements cannot be met, the system will alert the user of the shortfall.
Planning	The method requires creating movement plans with data entered by commodity and transportation planners or imported from other systems (example BCS3, TC-AIMS II, etc.). In the planning mode, system processing will take into account cargo dimensions and asset availability, and it will allocate resources according to the relevant rules (i.e., military to commercial). The method needs to provide the user

	with an option to accept, modify, or cancel a movement plan as generated.
Modeling	The method requires the creation of a convoy plan that adheres to stated theater movement policies and regulations.
Asset Allocation	The method needs to allocate assets according to cargo characteristics (e.g., weight, cube, and type).
	The method requires grouping these assets into serials and convoys, checking the availability of assets, and allocating the number of assets needed to move the cargo.
	The method needs to decrement assets from the available sources in accordance with the accepted transport plan, and it will account for allocated and planned assets to identify shortfalls and chart the results.
Sizing and Optimizing Capacity	The method entails building a recommended movement plan through optimization of cargo-to-asset assignment and time-distance calculations. The method is to be accomplished within the parameters of stated theater policies as input.
Data Analysis	The method needs to sort cargo from sea or air manifests by any of the identifying reference numbers (e.g., ULN, UIC, unit name, MSC).
	The method requires, in combination with a more comprehensive Common Usage Land Transportation (CULT) report and interaction with other transportation information systems, receiving advance notice of a shipment of cargo, checking the availability of assets, and building an estimate of the number and type of transport vehicles needed to continue the

	movement of that cargo. This will be accomplished within a framework of constraints from local command policy and theater directives. The method needs to generate the needed Transportation Movement Request (TMR) for tasking once a plan is accepted. The method requires reducing labor and time requirements by providing a fast and accurate movement-planning tool suitable for large and complex shipments of cargo. The system will save time for both transportation planners and customer units. The system will also eliminate errors in transcription and double handling of information through non-standard spreadsheet management.
Field Formats	The method requirements need to use input fields and formats that are currently used in theater and military manuals on cargo dimension standards. <u>Note</u>. Refer to technical bulletin TB 55-46-1 for a reference table on cargo dimensions.
Tracking Data for the Common Operating Picture (COP)	The method allows data to populate the logistical Common Operating Picture (COP) for ease of use in developing Op-Views (for tracking) and a projected "push matrix" (i.e., a distribution spreadsheet of movement and commodities within a 72-hour period).
Report Generation	The system will allow the user to generate printed movement plans and reports.
Development Platform	The method, if automated, requires development on a software and application independent platform that provides an easy interface with other systems.

Technical Requirements

If you were to decide to develop, an automated Capacity Management Tool to be relevant with the standards, then the Army has established you must adhere to the technical standards explained in these directives:

- DODI 8500.2:
http://www.dtic.mil/whs/directives/corres/pdf/850002p.pdf

- DODD 8500.1: https://www.cac.mil/assets/pdfs/DoDD_8500.1.pdf

- Army Regulation 25-2: http://www.fas.org/irp/doddir/army/ar25-2.pdf

I am not going to discuss in all the technical standards and requirements the need to create a tool, mainly since I do not have the skill set required to talk in-depth on the topic. My expertise is on the process development side of the house not the automated architecture required to create a working software and application itself. However, for the technically inclined I have provided some of the proper references and reading material required.

Functional Requirements

The Capacity Management methodology must process commodity and transport data, and allow the user to generate resource movement plans (Table 2; Functional Requirements).

Table 2: Functional Requirements

Feature	Description
Data Correlation Options	The method is required to provide the ability to combine asset and cargo sets into convoys in accordance with theater policies
User Interface	The method must provide the ability to accept user parameter input, by setting theater rules of engagement (ROE).

	The method needs to allow the user to add platforms and cargo dimensions as required. The method is required to provide the user with an option to accept, modify, or cancel the plan as generated (and manually build a convoy plan).
Display Format	The method used must provide the ability to create a projected convoy plan utilizing the Push Matrix format.
Data Sharing	The method is required to complete (i.e., "auto-fill") the Transportation Movement Request (TMR) so that it is ready for submission.

The method also needs to perform computations with formulas that accept data values supplied by the user. This will allow the user to accommodate different requirements for allocating assets to a wide range of cargo types (Table 3; Cargo Types).

Table 3: Cargo Types

Feature	Description
Cargo	Supplies, materials, stores, baggage, or equipment transported by land, water, or air.
Bulk	Dry or liquid cargo (water, fuel, oil, coal, grain, ore, sulfur, or fertilizer) shipped not in its own container, or unpacked in large quantities. In addition, this needs to encompass air cargo that fits with the dimensions of a 436L pallet with a design height of 96" for easy configuration of air platforms.
Containerized Cargo	This references those items that can be stowed or stuffed into a closed SEAVAN or MILVAN to protect the commodities shipped.
Non-Containerized	This references those items that cannot be stowed or stuffed into SEAVANs or MILVANs for shipment (i.e., over-

Cargo	dimensional or overweight cargo).
Oversize	This entails air cargo that exceeds the dimensions of bulk cargo but is equal to or less than 1,090" in length, 117" in width and 105" in height.
Outsize	This references that air cargo exceeding the dimensions of oversize cargo and requires the use of C-5 or C-17 aircraft.
Source Stuffed Cargo	This references cargo that economically fills a container from a single point of origin.

The method allows the user to adjust the data values used in the calculations, thereby making it possible to account for variable cargo characteristics such as weight, cube, and type. The user will then be able to create a convoy plan that is suitable to stated theater movement policies and regulations.

System Infrastructure

The Capacity Management methodology supports the planning function associated with the logistics movement infrastructure. The functional concept behind the Capacity Management procedure supports these objectives:

- The method must generate information for use in movement planning.

- The method is required to help standardize commodities and movement platforms into theater-configured loads.

- The commodity and movement managers will be able to set the configurations for the theater movement so that the cargo to move is arranged into a configuration that matches a platform that registered in the Common Usage Land Transportation (CULT) report.

Objectives, Metrics, and Benchmarks for Planning Loads and Convoys

The method allows managers to set and change the load and platform configurations. Method validation requirements are based on performance objectives related to the various phases of the convoy planning process (Table 4; Performance Objectives).

Table 4: Performance Objectives

Process Phase	Validation Objectives / Metrics / Benchmarks
Matching Cargo to Lift Opportunities	The method requires acceptance of data made available from other sources to make designated cargo eligible for an opportunity lift as identified in an analysis of existing convoy plans. The method needs to analyze all existing convoy plans, identify deadhead legs, and match cargo awaiting transportation en-route from existing Transportation Movement Requests (TMR) to find opportunities to add cargo. The method prioritizes all TMRs in accordance with theater movement priorities and Required Delivery Date (RDD). The method references an internal database of cargo dimensions and weights to compare cargo being transported to the carrying capacity (in both weight and cube) of the assets carrying them. It will compute the capacity left over with the capacity of empty trucks and compare that capacity with existing TMRs that are traveling to, or near to, the location of the cargo awaiting transport. (Note: TB 55-46-1 can be used as a reference table for cargo dimensions.)
Allocating Equipment for	The method allocates assets in a manner that takes into account variations in

Transport Needs	cargo characteristics (e.g., weight, cube, and type).
	The method groups those assets into serials and convoys, check availability of assets, and allocates the needed number of assets.
	The method then decrements assets from the available pool in accordance with the accepted plan and keeps account of allocated and planned assets to identify shortfalls and chart results.
Planning Loads and Convoys	The method must produce a convoy plan that meets stated theater movement policies and regulations.
	The method provides the user with an option to accept, modify, or cancel the plan as generated.
	The method must provide planners with the ability to sort cargo from sea or air manifests by any of the identifying reference numbers (e.g., ULN, UIC, unit name, and MSC).

	In combination with a more comprehensive CULT report and interactivity with other TIS, the method should perform these tasks:
	
	    — Receive advance notice of a shipment of cargo.
	
	    — Check the availability of assets.
	
	    — Build an estimate of the number and type of trucks needed to continue movement of the cargo based on a framework of restraints and constraints from

	local command policy and theater directives. The method provides various options to the planner to help frame the development of the convoy requirements (e.g., whether all cargo must move together or move as soon as possible, even if it is broken up into different shipments). The planner would be able to accept it in total, accept it with modifications, or decline to accept the plan.

Process Flow

The Capacity Management method processes data used to arrange convoys and alert the planner of available transport options. The process flow encompasses accessing information, analyzing the data, and generating output that maps out a recommended movement plan (See Figure 16; Capacity Management Method Functionality).

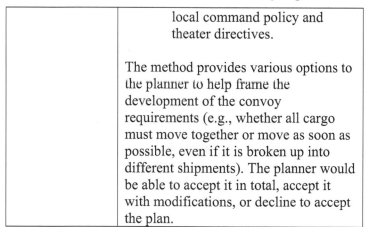

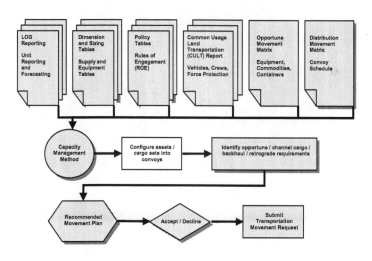

Figure 16; Capacity Management Method Functionality

Once a transportation plan is accepted, the manager must submit a Transportation Movement Request (TMR) to their local Movement Control Team (MCT) or Movement Control Battalion (MCB) to complete the process.

Data Analysis

Data analysis involves six data sources (Figure 17; Data Sources Associated with the Capacity Management Method). These data sources represent functions required to support a capacity management methodology either manual or automated.

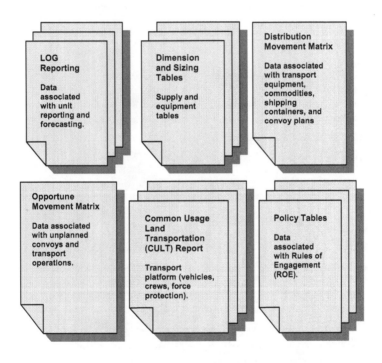

Figure 17; Data Sources Associated with the Capacity Management Method

Dimension and Sizing Tables

The dimension and sizing phase contains a series of tables that make it possible to configure types of supplies and equipment. The computations allow the user to change or add data associated with type, items, configurations, and quantities as required. The dimension and sizing file contains two types of conversion tables (Table 5; Commodity and Equipment Conversion Tables):

Table 5: Commodity and Equipment Conversion Tables

Commodity Configuration Conversion Factors	The factors in this table are based on unit of issues and other packing dimension data provided by the Federal Logistics Catalog (FEDLOG) or the Standard Army Retail Supply System (SARSS).
Equipment Conversion Factors	The factors in this table are based on the TB 55-46-1* reference table for cargo dimensions.

* (Army Technical Bulletin) TB 55-46-1. Standard Characteristics (Dimensions, Weight and Cube) for Transportability of Military Vehicles and Other Outsize/Overweight Equipment. 1 January 1991.

Motor Transport Planning

Motor transport planning involves application of the following factors (Table 6; Transport Planning Factors):

Table 6: Transport Planning Factors

Task Vehicle Availability Rate	This is the average number of assigned task vehicles that are not in maintenance and are currently available for daily mission support.
Vehicle Payload Capacity	This is the rated cargo capacity of the vehicle. During planning, the off-road payload capacity of the equipment is used to determine allowable highway load capacities.

Determining Transport and Vehicle Requirements

The method applies the following formulas to compute unit and vehicle requirements. These computations are based on planning estimates, actual operational data, or a combination of both (Table 7; Load and Transport Requirements). <u>Note</u>. The load must be computed with the appropriate commodity unit (e.g., STONs, containers, gallons).

Table 7: Load and Transport Requirements

Unit Lift Operations	A "unit lift" is the amount of cargo a trucking company or operation can move at one time (a one-time lift). The system uses the following formula to determine the number of vehicles or trucking operations needed to transport a given commodity in a unit lift: Required vehicles = $\frac{\text{Commodity quantity to be moved}}{\text{Capacity* per vehicle}}$ Required companies = $\frac{\text{Commodity quantity to be moved}}{\text{Capacity* per vehicle x average number of vehicles available per company}}$ * Appropriate commodity capacity (STONs, containers, gallons, etc.)
Specific Loads	A "specific load" consists of one or more items that have peculiarities or unique features that make it necessary to deviate from normal planning (i.e., to determine requirements for the vehicles needed in the operation). The items, for example, packed in a way that gives the package unusual size, shape, cube, or weight. In such cases, planners first attempt to determine vehicle requirements by test loading or by using operational data available from previous operations that involved similar circumstances. Sometimes, however, test loading is not feasible or operational data is unavailable.

In these cases, take the following steps to determine vehicle requirements:

1. Use this ratio to determine the number of items that may be loaded onto one vehicle by cargo weight:

> Vehicle payload capacity
> Weight of item to be transported

2. Use this ratio to determine the number of items that may be loaded onto one vehicle by cube capacity:

> Vehicle compartment capacity
> Cube of item to be transported

If the value using cargo weight is the lesser value, then the weight of the computed load will exceed the vehicle's payload capacity before all available compartment space is filled.

If the value using cargo cube is the lesser value, the computed cargo load will "cube out" (i.e., exceed the cubic cargo space available in the vehicle) before it "weighs out" (i.e., exceed the vehicle payload capacity).

3. Determine the number of vehicles required to transport the load based on mission need (onetime lift or daily-sustained operation).

Number of items to be transported
Number of items that can be transported per vehicle

(Select the lesser value yielded by Steps 1 and 2)

	<u>Note</u>: The vehicle payload and compartment cube capacity can be obtained from the vehicle data plate. The weight and cubic volume of a specific item or load can be obtained from the shipper or service representative.

Commodity Configuration Conversion Factors Table

The method references the Commodity Configuration Conversion Factors table to perform calculations that involve a variety of commodities (Table 8; Commodity Configuration Conversion Factors with Sample Supply Items). Any commodity and conversion factors can be added from FEDLOG or from data entered by the user.

* Note: The following conversion factors are only examples of numbers to depict the overall theory of the concept of configuring loads to fit the movement platform. If you have numbers that are more relevant then please replace. The conversion tables are design to be adjusted or giving the capability to add commodities and/or equipment. The factors for containers are a 20' Container (16 pallets), or 40' Container (32 pallets).

Table 8: Commodity Configuration Conversion Factors with Sample Supply Items

Supply Class	Item	Unit/ Issue	Units/ Pallet	463L Pallet	20' Container /max W 6.47 tons	40' Container /max W 15.42 tons	Calculation Formula
Class I	MRE	12 / case	48 / cases	192 / cases	768 / cases	1536 / cases	Commodity quantity required = Number of commodity Commodity Configuration capacity required
	UGR	50 / mod.	8 / mod.	32 / mod.	128 / mod.	256 / mod.	
	HCP	300 / case	6 / cases	24 / cases	96 / cases	192 / cases	
	Bottle Water	12 / case	48 / cases	192 / cases	768 / cases	1536 / cases	

Table 8. Commodity Configuration Conversion Factors with Sample Supply Items

	Item	Unit/ Issue	Units/ Pallet	463L Pallet	20' Container /max W 6.47 tons	40' Container /max W 15.42 tons	Calculation Formula
Class II	Canister, filter, mask	10 / box	50 box	200 box	800 box	1600 box	Commodity quantity required = Number of Commodity Configuration / commodity capacity required
	Suit, protective	20 / box	2 box	8 box	32 box	64 box	

Table 8: Commodity Configuration Conversion Factors with Sample Supply Items

Supply Class	Item	Unit/ Issue	Units/ Pallet	463L Pallet	20' Container /max W 6.47 tons	40' Container /max W 15.42	Calculation Formula
Class III (P)	Seal Grease 20 lb can	6 / box	8 box	32 box	128 box	256 box	Commodity quantity required = Number of Commodity Configuration commodity capacity required
	Gear oil 90 wt Qt can	12 / case	16 cases	64 cases	256 cases	512 cases	

Table 8: Commodity Configuration Conversion Factors with Sample Supply Items

Supply Class	Item	Unit/ Issue	Units/ Pallet	463L Pallet	20' Container /max W 6.47 tons	40' Container /max W 15.42 tons	Calculation Formula
Class IV	Barbed wire, 50 ft	1 rolls	50 rolls	200 rolls	800 rolls	1600 rolls	Commodity quantity required = Number of commodity capacity required / Commodity Configuration
	Concertina, barb tape 25 ft	1 rolls	50 rolls	200 rolls	800 rolls	1600 rolls	

Table 8: Commodity Configuration Conversion Factors with Sample Supply Items

Supply Class	Item	Unit/ Issue	Items/ Unit	Units/ Pallet	463L Pallet	20' Container /max W 6.47 tons	40' Container /max W 15.42 tons	Calculation Formula
Class V	A059 - 5.56mm ball	Box	1680 boxes	48 boxes	192 boxes	768 boxes	1536 boxes	Commodity quantity required = Number of Commodity Configuration commodity capacity required
	A131 - 7.62 mm linked	Box	800 boxes	40 boxes	160 boxes	720 boxes	1440 boxes	
	A576 - .50 cal linked	Box	200 boxes	48 boxes	192 boxes	768 boxes	1536 boxes	

Table 8: Commodity Configuration Conversion Factors with Sample Supply Items

Supply Class	Item	Unit/ Issue	Military Tanks	Commercial Tanks	Tank, Portable fabric	Type 1 Railroad tank car	Type 2 Railroad tank car	Type 3 Railroad tank car	Calculation Formula
Class III (Bulk)	JP8	Gal	5000	7500	10000	8000	10000	12000	Commodity quantity required = Number of Commodity Configuration commodity capacity required
	MO GAS	Gal	5000	7500	10000	8000	10000	12000	
	DF2	Gal	5000	7500	10000	8000	10000	12000	

Equipment Configuration Conversion Factors Table

The method uses the Equipment Configuration Conversion Factors table to perform calculations involving equipment platforms (Table 9; Equipment Configuration Conversion Factors with Sample Supply Items). Any equipment and conversion factors can be added from TB 55-46-1 as a reference table for cargo dimensions or from supporting data entered by the user.

* Note: The following conversion factors are only examples of numbers to depict the overall theory of the concept of configuring loads to fit the movement platform. If you have numbers that are more relevant then please replace. The conversion tables are design to be adjusted or to provide the capability to add commodities and/or equipment. The factors for containers are a 20' Container (16 pallets), or 40' Container (32 pallets).

Table 9: Equipment Configuration Conversion Factors with Sample Supply Items

Equipment Hauling Platforms	Weight	Capacity of Pallets	Capacity Per Platform of 463L Pallets	Capacity Per Platform of 20' Container / max W 6.47 tons	Capacity Per Platform of 40' Container / max W 15.42 tons	Calculation Formula
30' Trailer	10000 LBS	18	3	1	0	
40' Trailer	20000 LBS	32	4	2	1	$\dfrac{\textit{Number of Commodity Capacity required}}{\textit{Capacity per vehicle x average number of vehicles}} = $ *Number of Vehicles Required*
PLS	16.5 STONS / 16,102	10	2	1	0	
PLS Trailer	16.5 STONS / 16,102	10	2	1	0	

Table 9: Equipment Configuration Conversion Factors for Class III (B) Supplies with Sample Supply Items

Equipment Hauling Platforms	Weight	Capacity of JP8	Capacity MOGAS	Capacity DF2	Calculation Formula
Military Tanker	15.3 STONS	5,000 GALS	5,000 GALS	5,000 GALS	
Commercial Tanker	23.6 STONS	7,500 GALS	7,500 GALS	7,500 GALS	
Tank, portable Fabric	30.6 STONS	10,000 GALS	10,000 GALS	10,000 GALS	<u>Number of Commodity Capacity required</u> = Number of Vehicles Required
Type 1 Railroad Tank car	24.1 STONS	8,000 GALS	8,000 GALS	8,000 GALS	Capacity per vehicle x average Number of vehicles
Type 2 Railroad Tank car	30.6 STONS	10,000 GALS	10,000 GALS	10,000 GALS	
Type 3 Railroad Tank car	36.8 STONS	12,000 GALS	12,000 GALS	12,000 GALS	

Policy Parameter Data

The method uses established Policy Parameter data to perform calculations associated with Policies and Rules of Engagement (ROE) (Table 10; Policy Parameter Data Factors with Sample Supply Items). These entries represent examples of types of information required and can be replaced to support your operational requirements.

Table 10: Policy Parameter Data Factors with Sample Supply Items

Data Field	Minimum Platforms	Maximum Platforms	Ratio Platforms W	Ratio Platforms G	Times Start	End	Routes	Calculation
Convoy Platform Density	5	30	23	5	TBD	TBD	TBD	Convoy Platform Density = no > 30 and not< 5
Convoy Protection Platform (CPP)	2	4	TBD	2	TBD	TBD	TBD	Convoy Protection Platform (CPP) = no > than 4 and not < 2
Convoy Platform Ratio of Commercial and Military	2	30	23	5	TBD	TBD	TBD	Convoy Platform Ratio of Commercial and Military = CPP + Ratio W + Ratio G = (= to or < than) Maximum Convoy Platform Density
Route Black-Out Alert	TBD	TBD	TBD	TBD	TBD	TBD	TBD	Start + End = Route Black-Out Alert / Route

Using the CULT File to Assess Transport Equipment Availability

The method requires the usage of some type of reference report depicting status of a units Common Usage Land Transportation (CULT) report to manage transport platforms (i.e., vehicles and crews) and to evaluate Convoy Protection Platform availability. This makes it possible to report availability by unit and type and to display data for review. The user would query the different unit reports (i.e., the CULT files) and identify available platforms that are eligible for tasking. The analysis may generate output that recommends the creation of new convoys or the addition of platforms to existing convoys. A designated single manager who is responsible for all motor carrier cargo movements in a theater, specific country, or geographic region manages the process. The theater combatant commander usually designates the predominant component as the CULT manager.

The process is summarized as follows:

1. Allocate transport assets according to cargo characteristics such as weight, cube, and type.

2. Group these assets into serials and convoys.

3. Check the availability of transport equipment.

The system applies this formula:

$$\frac{\text{Number of Commodity Capacity Required}}{\text{Capacity per vehicle x average number of vehicles available per company on CULT}} = \text{Required Vehicles Available}$$

4. Allocate the needed number of assets.

5. Decrement assets from the available pool in accordance with the accepted plan, and keep account of allocated and planned assets to identify shortfalls and chart results.

Process Flow and Data Sources

The Capacity Management methodology requires the manager to analyze cargo and equipment data and generate a transport plan for the operation. The capacity management method is multi-faceted. It encompasses planning, analyzing, sizing, optimizing, and managing cargo and transport equipment capacity to satisfy resource demand in a timely manner. The process involves accessing several information sources (See Figure 18; Transport Planning Information Sources).

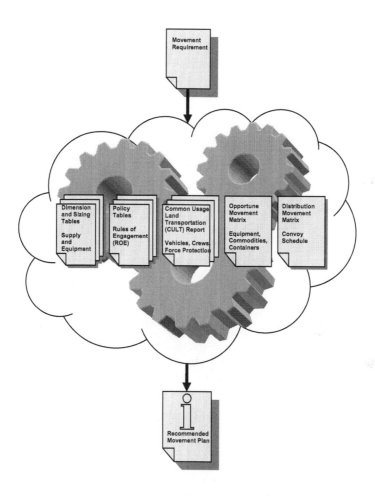

Figure 18; Transport Planning Information Sources

The method provides a series of checks and balances between different data sources. The manager must establish business rules that all involved adhere to so the factors provided will police the method functions. This process involves five information sources (See Figure 19; Process Flow for the Capacity Management Methodology).

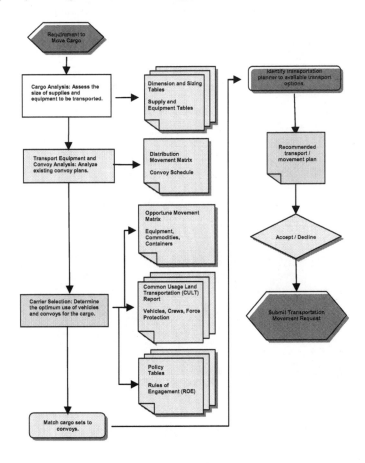

Figure 19; Process Flow for the Capacity Management Methodology

The capacity management methodology encompasses six phases:

- <u>Sizing</u> - Assessing the size of supplies and equipment

- <u>Analyzing</u> - Analyzing existing convoy plans
- <u>Optimizing</u> - Optimizing the utilization of vehicles and convoys

- <u>Managing</u> - Managing cargo transport plans

- Planning - Planning cargo loads for convoys

Dimension and Sizing

The Dimension and Sizing phase consists of a series of tables that make it possible to configure types of supplies and transport equipment (See Figure 20).

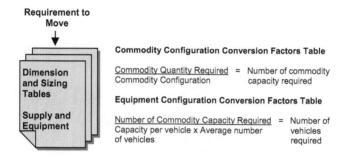

Figure 20; Requirement to Move Calculation

Distribution Movement Matrix

In this phase, se the manager analyzes all existing convoy plans and compares the cargo awaiting transit to the carrying capacity of the convoy (Figure 21).

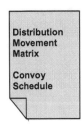

✓ Analyze all existing convoy plans, identify deadhead legs, and match cargo awaiting transportation en route (using data from existing TMRs) to find opportunities to add cargo.

✓ Compare the volume of cargo being transported to the carrying capacity of available assets or amount of platforms per convoy.

✓ Compute the capacity of empty platforms or the capacity available on partially loaded platforms (or indicated on existing TMRs) that are in transit to or near the location of the cargo awaiting transportation.

Figure 21; Matching Cargo to Convoys

Opportune Movement Matrix

In this phase, the manager identifies any opportune movement eligible for incorporation into the plan (Figure 22).

✓ Identify available lift opportunities for which the cargo is eligible (i.e., for assignment to existing convoy plans).

✓ Notify the planner of a potential lift opportunity (based on location, priority, and RDD) and offer the option to assign the load to the existing convoy plan.

Figure 22; Convoy Plan Analysis

Common Usage Land Transportation (CULT)

In this phase, the manager performs queries against the Common Usage Land Transportation (CULT) report to identify available transport platforms. These platforms are used to form recommendations for creating new convoys or adding platforms to existing convoys (Figure 23).

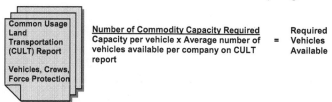

Figure 23; Data Analysis Formula for the CULT

Policy Parameter Data

In this phase, the manager references the Policy Parameter Data to ensure that movement plans conform to established policies and Rules of Engagement (Figure 24).

Figure 24; Rules of Engagement and the Policy Parameter Data

Planning Convoys

In this phase, the manager combines asset / cargo sets into convoys in accordance with theater policies (Figure 25).

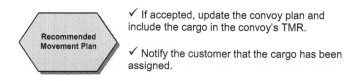

Figure 25; Movement Plan Determination

The manager updates the convoy plan and uses the cargo data to populate the convoy's Transportation Movement Request (TMR).

LTC James H. Henderson, "Cotton", USA (Ret.)

To sum up the capacity management methodology it is a method to easily analyze reported data on commodity and movement capabilities, and provides a way to calculate the requirements to develop a plan of operation that supports sustainment.

Planning

Chapter 9

Military Decision Making Process (MDMP)

Concept

There are many types of plan concepts. There are financial plans, house plans, strategic plans, vacation plans, just to name a few. Whatever the reason to develop a plan, there is one constant point and that is to make something happen. No matter who you are, or what you do, everyone conducts some sort of planning throughout our day-to-day life. How well we perform the development is the key to building an executable plan with a successful outcome. Decision-making, when performed correctly, can provide the answer to difficult problems, issues, and/or situations. There are many forms of the decision-making process used throughout the world, but I will discuss only three, the *Basic Problem Solving Model*, the *Military Decision Making Process (MDMP)*, and *Staff Estimates*. When implementing either process you must remember that the decision-making process needs formalization. Staff elements frequently change personnel leading to a lack of continuity within the staff structure. By identifying a common framework to conduct planning and decision-making under, you have laid the foundation that facilitates the integration of new personnel and provides the capability to add organizations even as the process is in progress without causing set backs or turmoil.

Basic Problem Solving Model

To conduct simple decision-making the best procedure is the Basic Problem Solving Model.

Basic Problem Solving Model

1. **Identify the Problem**

2. **Develop Solutions**

3. **Compare Alternatives**

4. **Decision**

This procedure has four straightforward elements. The first is to *"Identify the Problem"*. This is not as easy as it may seem. What looks like the problem may only be the face value and sometimes what appears to be the problem is only one of many issues. Until you identify all the issues, do you really see the problem to resolve? The second is to *"Develop Solutions"* where you extend options or alternatives that provide answers that might solve the problem. This is the most important phase of the model in that during this phase of the process you begin to develop courses of action that could give a solution to the problem. The third element is to *"Compare Alternatives"*. This is the process of calculating approximately the alternatives. At this phase of the procedure, all options are evaluated against subjective criteria and ranked to determine their relevance. The fourth is self-explanatory; it is the *"Decision"* that is made after all the above is completed.

Military Decision Making Process and *Staff Estimate*

The military does the best job with planning of any organization I know. They have training courses designed just to instruct leaders in the art of decision-making, and this training taught is the Military Decision Making Process (MDMP) and Staff Estimates. The process educates their leaders in decision-making and Course of Action (COA) development. Utilizing the process, they construct complex plans to synchronize multiple units in the execution of a phased combat operation, as well as contingency plans. It has often been said, "That the Army had future operations staffs concerned only with the question *"What If"*, and their only purpose in life is to build contingency plans." I do not know if this is true, but the philosophy is what we need to propagate as we begin to research and develop logistical support plans. This is because these plans have to lay out courses of action and contingence plans that provide different options to a scenario that is very uncertain pertaining to support timeframe, unit density, and missions. The plan has to be so complete that no matter the diversity there are always options described in detail for higher headquarters and their subordinate units to coordinate and synchronize so that the execution is almost automatic in nature. Let us review this procedure called the Military Decision Making Process (MDMP) and Staff Estimates.

LTC James H. Henderson, "Cotton", USA (Ret.)

- **Military Decision Making Process (MDMP)** - is a standard planning decision-making model. Key components of MDMP are:

  - Receive mission
  - Mission analysis
  - Course of Action development
  - COA Analysis
  - COA Comparison
  - COA Approval
  - Orders Production

- **Estimates** - are formal processes used to analyze a problem from a specific functional area, providing an in depth staff analysis of the situation. There are two types of estimates, and the reason for the two different estimates is the time given to provide a solution or at least start some sort of action to give time for further analysis.

  - **Commander's Estimate** provides for a broader outlook on the situation, by conducting a general analysis of a problem, rather than a detailed analysis. The Commander's Estimate offers an autonomous analysis of a problem and in turn a quicker solution to start to implement.

  - **Staff Estimate** is a modified problem analysis method geared to specific staff agencies or a particular functional area of expertise. The Staff Estimate guarantees that all aspects of problem and its related issues are analyzed in detail so follow on staff coordination and synchronization can happen. Staff element examples:

    - Operations
    - Logistics
    - Medical
    - Maintenance
    - Transportation
    - Etc.

To provide for the limited time factor required to begin execution, as well as to conduct detailed analysis needed to develop a complete plan the incorporation of both procedures is required. To achieve the proper outcome and solution, the two processes are equally supportive of one another in they that provide for a quick execution of some tasks (Specified

96

Tasks), while other staff elements are conducting detail analysis of other tasks, as well as lead to additional planning, coordination, synchronization, and execution related to specific functional areas (Implied Tasks). So let us review the seven components of the Military Decision Making Process (MDMP)

- **Receive Mission** – is normally self-explanatory, but the bottom line is something has happened and some sort of reaction is required *"Who, What, When, Where, and Why,"* are all part of the problem to be resolved. Therefore, the staff must conduct an initial assessment, consisting of staff estimates, to prepare for Mission Analysis.

- **Mission analysis** – accurately defines the problem *"Who, What, When, Where, and Why,"* needing to be resolved. At times, the problem statement is easily recognized, but other times it is very hard to understand. One objective is that the mission statement provides organizational focus. The key to a good Mission Analysis is a clearly defined mission statement. The following are important steps of the Mission Analysis process:

  - Analyze available documentation
    - Operations Orders
    - Standard Operating Procedures (SOPs)
    - Verbal guidance
    - Polices
    - Regulations
    - Any other relevant documents
    - Maps / Terrain

  - Determine: specified / implied / essential tasks

  - Review available assets

  - Determine constraints

  - Identify critical facts and assumptions

  - Determine initial recon requirements

  - Plan use of available time

  - Develop restated mission

- Conduct mission analysis brief

- Approve restated mission

- Develop initial, proposed intent

- Issue guidance

- Issue warning order

- Review facts / assumptions

• **Course of Action (COA) development** – identifies acceptable options that if implemented accomplish the mission or resolve the problem. Each COA considered must be suitable (can accomplish the mission), feasible (within capabilities of organization, subordinate units, or commercial venders), acceptable (means justify the ends), distinguishable (each COA must be distinctly different from others), and have completeness (an inclusive review of all options). The following are steps to develop COAs:

- Analyze relative capabilities
- Create options

- Identify organization, agencies, or commercial venders

- Develop scheme of execution

- Assign organization / agencies / commercial venders

- Prepare COA statements / diagrams

• **COA Analysis** – is the implementation of a detailed study of each COA. This procedure analyzes all the data provided and organizes it in such away that the results provide you with the ability to compare each COA. The following are steps to COA Analysis:

- Assemble the tools
    - Maps/pictures/terrain analysis products
    - COA diagrams
    - Synchronization Matrixes

  – Event Templates
  – Staff estimates

- List all organization, subordinate units, or commercial venders

- List assumptions
  – Are they still valid, and relevant
  – Need to make any additional assumptions
  – Have any new information that validates existing assumptions

- List known critical events and decision points
  – Critical events are actions you know or anticipate occurring that warrant detailed analysis
  – Decision Points are actions you know or anticipate that may require a significant decision

- Determine evaluation criteria
  – What criteria to analyze and compare each COA
  – How to quantify each criterion

- Select war-game method
  – Belt technique - analyzes and synchronizes all activities in a given area, very time consuming
  – Box technique - analyzes all activities in a selected area, very detailed and focused, and a good technique in time-constrained environment. This technique prioritizes events down to just a few to evaluate, and ignores other events to then be reviewed at another time
  – Avenues in depth - analyze all activities from start to finish along a given path. This procedure is very detailed and time consuming

- Select method to record and display results
  – Synchronization Matrix – develops a planning tool that you will require later to assist in coordination and rehearsals. This procedure is a detailed synchronization of events and is time consuming
  – Sketch note method is faster; less detailed, and development of a synchronization matrix is required later

- War-game actions and assess results

- Must be realistic
- Action and counter-action
- Remain unbiased
- List advantages and disadvantages (as found)
- Continually assess COA feasibility, acceptability, and suitability
- Avoid drawing premature conclusions and gathering facts to support such conclusions
- Compare COAs during comparison process: "Not during war game"

• **COA Comparison** – determines decision criteria and assigns weighting values to criteria
- Be as objective as possible
- Assess Risk
- Make recommendation

• **COA Approval** – upon completion of COAs development, evaluation, and staff has come to a recommendation, they then conduct a decision brief laying out the plan
- Select COA
- Assess Risk
- Specify Type of Order

• **Orders Production** – publication of written order and guidance in the form of a document plan which is then sent out to all players involved:
- Translate into Plan / Order
- Incorporate Branches and Sequels
- Establish Control Measures
- Synchronize Plan / Order

The last phase of the process is conducting a good rehearsal so all players both understand and can execute their portion of the plan. There are five types of rehearsal the Confirmation Brief, Back Brief, Operational Events Rehearsal, Support Rehearsal, Task or Standard Operating Procedure (SOP) Rehearsal. The two that are most important in my opinion, are the Operational Events and the Support Rehearsals, because they bring all the players to the table that facilitate coordination and synchronization. When operating in a constrained planning time environment the outcome is usually when you need more time or information and you get less, and when you need less information and involvement you tend to get more.

Planning in Time Constrained Environment	Require	Acquire
Available Planning Time	More	Less
Level of Supervisor Involvement	Less	More
Detail in Supervisor Guidance	Less	More
Flexibly and Latitude of Staff	More	Less
Number of COA Developed	More	Less
Detailed Operations Order to Publish	More	Less

The above table is usually the norm of most planning situations. Practice and understanding of the decision-making process can drastically reduce planning time.

Theory and Execution

So now, let us provide an example of the process in use, the problem – *"there is a requirement for a M1A1 tank engine"*. I will demonstrate the **Basic Problem Solving Model**:

1. Identify the Problem – I need a M1A1 tank engine

2. Develop Solutions - what are my options,

    - Local Supply Support Activity (SSA)
        - On-hand
        - No Due-outs
        - Customer
    - Controlled Substitution
    - Cross level from other units

3. Compare Alternatives – availability, time, distance, movement, labor, reliability, etc.

4. Decision – On-hand with no due-outs at local SSA, so drop a requisition for one M1A1 tank engine and deliver to required unit.

The process just explained is good for uncomplicated problems and issues, but for scenarios that are more complex, we need to use a process that allows for more analysis and estimates that identify all the problems, and collects the issues for resolution. Here is an example of what I am discussing. The problem is *"the Support Operations Officer (SPO) receives a mission from higher headquarters directing resupply of ammunition (Class V) to Forward Operating Base (FOB) ATLANTA, a support base within the Brigades area of responsibility, within the next 24 hour support cycle . You are located on Logistical Support Area (LSA) JACKSON."* The problem is big enough just to find the proper amount of ammunition to support the mission, but there are added issues associated with the problem that complicate the situation even more like location, distance, time, priority of support, availability of commodity, availability of movement assets, convoy rules of engagement (ROE), route status, and force protection, just to name a few. The additional issues that complicate the problem are *specified, implied, and essential tasks*, and they need solving along with the problem, or they, too will become problems. Specified tasks you are directed to do. Implied tasks you must do, but are not necessarily directed to do, and Essential tasks must be accomplished or risk failure. Remember essential tasks can align under either specified or implied tasks. The following is an example if you tried to use the Basic Problem Solving Model:

1. **Identify the Problem** – Resupply of ammunition (Class V) to FOB ATLANTA, within the next 24 hour support cycle

2. **Develop Solutions** - what are my options

   a. **Options,**

      1) Local Supply Support Activity (SSA)
         - On-hand
         - No Due-outs
         - Customer

      2) Cross level from other units

      3) Support from LSA JACKSON in theater

      4) Support from another FOB or LSA in an adjacent region in theater

5) Support from outside theater resources

6) Combination of any or all of the above

b. **Additional Questions**,

1) What is the priority of support in theater?

2) What is the availability of commodity within theater?

3) What is the availability of commodity outside of theater?

4) What is the number of available movement platforms by support units within theater?

5) What is the number of available movement platforms outside theater (Channel Flights or Green Ramp for example)?

6) What is the route status of the Distribution Network leading to that location?

7) What other supplies or resources are required (propellants, fuses, MHE, manpower)?

c. **Tasks**,

1) **Specified**: Resupply of ammunition (Class V) to FOB ATLANTA, within the next 24 hour support cycle

   a) **Essential**: Availability of commodity within theater

   b) **Essential**: Support Time Definite Deliver (TDD)

2) **Implied**:

   a) **Implied**: Priority of Support

      (1) Available stocks

         (a) **Essential:** Determine number of cases

(b) **Essential**: Determine whether there is an adequate supply of ammunition within theater

(c) **Essential**: Use LOG Reporting Data Information Displays

(d) **Essential**: Evaluate On-Hand Stock Status Reports, with no due-outs

(e) **Essential:** Support from outside theater resources

(2) Reliable customer base

(a) **Essential:** Unit customer of SSA

(b) **Essential**: Commodity manager must call SSA to execute a *"file or kill"* requisition

b) **Implied**: Provide movement Platforms

(1) Submission of Transportation Movement Request (TMR)

(2) Validation of TMR that meets timeframe

(3) Equipment

(a) **Essential**: Determine transports required to make the move

(b) **Essential**: Evaluate Common
User Land Transport Report (CULT) for availability movement platforms (ground) in theater

(c) **Essential**: Evaluate Common
User Land Transport Report (CULT) for available movement platforms (ground) outside theater

(d) **Essential**: Evaluate Common
User Land Transport Report (CULT) for available crews

(e) **Essential:** Determine which unit will provide those (CULT reports)

(f) **Essential:** Evaluate availability of Intra-theater air

(g) **Essential:** Evaluate availability of Channel Flights (Strata-air)

(4) Loading commodity

(a) **Essential**: Project available staging, spotting, and loading times

(b) **Essential**: Available personnel

(c) **Essential:** Available Material Handling Equipment (MHE), example forklifts, Rich, K-loader, etc.

c) **Implied:** Conduct Resource Optimization

(1) Review Distribution Matrixes for opportune movement for space on existing projected platforms

(2) Review Distribution Matrixes for opportunity to add new platforms to convoys not over the ROE limit.

d) **Implied:** Evaluate Route Status

(1) Use Route Status (MSR/ASR) Data Information Displays

(2) Designate available route and spot time that meets TTD

e) **Implied:** Availability of Force Protection platforms and security

(1) Availability of gun trucks by location

(2) Availability of security windows

(2) MCT will notify the Transportation Company and the group providing security and designate a Spot Time that meets TTD

1) **Compare Alternatives** –   Dilemma is the list of Issues (Contingency Circumstances) – Implied Tasks are as big and overwhelming as the original Problem – Specified Task.

Problem – Specified Tasks	Issues (Contingency Circumstances) – Implied Tasks
Find ammunition (Class V) within the next 24 hours	Priority of Support
	Provide movement Platforms
	Conduct Resource Optimization
	Evaluate Route Status
	Availability of Force Protection platforms and security

Answer: You must develop a process that can solve the immediate Specified Task, as well as capture and work the list of Implied Tasks. The Basic Problem Solving Model is not designed to handle complex problems.

2) **Decision – "No decision made"?**   Find a way to get the Implied Tasks worked separately, by technical people, while the overall Specified Task is worked.

Therefore, to handle the complex problems and issues that are associated with logistical support operations we will require a more in depth process.

Military Decision Making Process and *Staff Estimate*

So now, let us work the above problem utilizing the Military Decision Making Process (MDMP) and Staff Estimates.

1. **Receive mission** - Resupply of ammunition (Class V) to FOB ATLANTA, within the next 24 hour support cycle

2. **Mission analysis** - "Who, What, When, Where, and Why," and clearly define mission statement.

Restated Mission Statement:

As of 112120FEB08, insurgent mortar attack has destroyed warehouse facilities that house Class V (Ammunition) at FOB Atlanta. Higher headquarter as directed emergency resupply of two DOS (Days of Supply) from an installation within unit's area of responsibility, to FOB ATLANTA, by 1800 hours on the following day.

3. **Course of Action development** - options,

   1) Local Supply Support Activity (SSA)
      - On-hand
      - No Due-outs
      - Customer

   2) Cross level from other units
   3) Support from LSA JACKSON in theater

   4) Support from another FOB or LSA in an adjacent region in theater

   5) Support from outside theater resources

   6) Combination of any or all of the above

4. **COA Analysis** - analyzes data and organizes,

Conduct Cdr Estimate	Conduct Staff Estimate
⬇	⬇
Problem – Specified Tasks	Issues (Contingency Circumstances) – Implied Tasks
⬇	⬇

Find (Class V) next 24 hours	Priority of Support
	Provide movement Platforms
	Conduct Resource Optimization
	Evaluate Route Status
	Availability of Force Protection platforms and security

5. **COA Comparison** – assign criteria and values,

COA #s	Flexibility	Simplicity	Capability	C2	Totals
1) Local SSA	1	2	0	2	5
2) Cross Level	1	1	0	1	3
3) Support from LSA JACKSON	1	2	3	1	7
4) Support from another FOB or LSA in an adjacent region in theater	1	2	2	1	6
5) Support from outside theater resources	1	1	1	1	4
6) Combination of any or all of the above	2	0	2	1	5

6. **COA Approval** - make recommendation,

COA #3 - Support from LSA JACKSON

7. **Orders Production** - publication of written order and guidance in the form of a document plan, and sent out to all players involved.

The above is a simple depiction of the procedures required to accomplish a complex problem, in reality it would take a lot more time and staff involvement to complete a plan that would support a problem of this magnitude. The next four chapters continue the analysis by taking the above situation and breaking it down by process phases (Planning and Preparation, Execution, Analysis, and Documentation) and depict how a Support Operations Officer would utilize the different staff sections to produce a solution to the situation. This, of course, is just an example and may not be the only way to accomplish the task, but does provide a good solution and model to evaluate and study.

Chapter 10

Planning and Preparation

Concept

Military planning is a process utilized for problem solving and decision-making. The process supports the commander in making decisions. The first phase, of the MDMP, is *"Planning and Preparation"* and includes the two key aspects to a successful execution. Sometimes there is the opportunity to use MDMP, supported by a complete staff, to create a fully developed and written order. But sometimes, time does not permit the full process and requires an abbreviated version. Therefore, the MDMP process is a combination of two methods: analytic and intuitive decision-making.

- Analytic decision-making is a more systematic look when a staff has more time, but does not work well in all situations, especially during execution, where conditions frequently require immediate decisions.

- Intuitive decision-making is the process of developing a solution based on previous experiences, knowledge, judgment, and perception focusing on assessment of the situation rather than assessment of options. This process works best in time-constrained situations.

Both techniques have its merit, but to pick one over the other depends on how much time and information are available. The analytic approach is suitable when time is available to review different courses of action (COA), or if a staff is inexperienced. The Intuitive process is used mainly during execution, when time and information are short.

Theory and Execution

Now let us say we are the Support Operations Officer (SPO) working in an operational level, sustainment staff position, and demonstrate how he/she would utilize the different staff sections to work the follow situation.

Step 1: Receipt of Mission:

"The Support Operations Officer (SPO) receives a mission from higher headquarters directing resupply of ammunition (Class V) to Forward Operating Base (FOB) ATLANTA, a support base within the Brigades area of responsibility, within the next 24 hour support cycle . You are located on Logistical Support Area (LSA) JACKSON."

Name	National Stock Number (NSN)	Number Rounds Required
A059 - 5.56mm ball	1305-01-155-5459	840,000 rds
A131 - 7.62 mm linked	1305-00-892-2150	160,000 rds
A576 - .50 cal linked	1305-00-028-6603	20,000 rds

Step 2: Mission Analysis:

Restated Mission Statement:

As of 112120FEB08, insurgent mortar attack has destroyed warehouse facilities that house Class V (Ammunition) at FOB Atlanta. Higher headquarter has directed emergency resupply of two DOS (Days of Supply) from an installation within unit's area of responsibility, to FOB ATLANTA, by 1800 hours on the following day.

Planning Data

Item	Unit/ Issue	Items/ Unit	Units/ Pallet	Weight/Unit (pounds)
A059 - 5.56mm ball	Box	1,680	48	67
A131 - 7.62 mm linked	Box	800	40	77
A576 - .50 cal linked	Box	200	48	77

Item	Unit/ Issue	Items/ Unit	Units/ Pallet	463L Pallet	20' Container /max W 6.47 tons	40' Container /max W 15.42 tons	Calculation Formula
A059 - 5.56mm ball	Box	1,680	48	192	768	1536	Commodity quantity required = Number of Commodity Configuration commodity capacity

							required
A131 - 7.62 mm linked	Box	800	40	160	720	1440	
A576 - .50 cal linked	Box	200	48	192	768	1536	

No. of Pallets:
LMTV (6 pallets)
MTV (8 pallets)
HEMTT (8 pallets)
M871 Trailer (12 pallets)　(1- 20' Container)
M872 Trailer (18 pallets)　(2 - 20' Containers)
PLS Flat-rack (10 pallets)　(1- 20' Container)

Calculation Formula
Number of Commodity Capacity required = Number of Vehicles Capacity per vehicle x average　　　　　　Required number of vehicles

Step 3: COA Development:

The Support Operations Officer disseminates tasks to the different staff sections for Plan Development:

Develop Plan

Staff Section: SPO Commodity Manager (Class V)	
Task: Priority of Support	Answers
(1) Available stocks	Yes
(a) Determine number of cases	A059 - 500 boxes A131 - 200 boxes A576 - 100 boxes
(b) Determine whether there is an adequate supply of ammunition within theater	LSA JACKSON
(c) Use LOG Reporting Data Information Displays (automated or analog)	Yes
(d) Evaluate On-Hand Stock Status Reports, with no due-outs	Quantity On-hand with no Due-outs
(e) Support from outside theater resources	Yes (Time permit?)
(2) Reliable customer base	No

(a) Is the unit a customer of SSA?	No
(b) If not - Commodity manager must call SSA to execute a "file or kill" requisition	Yes

Staff Section: Transportation Section				
Task: Provide movement Platforms	**Answers**			
(1) Submission of Transportation Movement Request (TMR)	Yes			
(2) Validation of TMR that meets timeframe	Yes			
(3) Equipment				
(a) Determine transports required to make the move	A059-500 box- 11pallets A131-200 box- 5 pallets A576-100 box- 3 pallets Total pallets= 19	4 LMTV or 3 MTV or 3 HEMTT or 2 M871 Trailer or 2 M872 Trailer or 2 PLS Flat-rack or	A059-500 box- 3 463L pallets A131-200 box- 2 463L pallets A576-100bx- 3 463L pallets Total pallets= 8	8 LMTV or 8 MTV or 4 HEMTT or 3 M871 or 2 M872 or 4 PLS or
(b) Evaluate Common User Land Transport Report (CULT) for available movement platforms (ground) in theater	Unit LMTV MTV HEMTT M871 M872 PLS - TL 3 SUS 2 9 24 23 40 10 6 12 SUS 0 0 0 46 50 0 0 6 SUS 4 6 12 20 43 0 0			
(c) Evaluate Common User Land Transport Report (CULT) for available movement platforms (ground) outside theater	Unit LMTV MTV HEMTT M871 M872 PLS - TL 4 SUS 0 0 0 70 60 0 0			
(d) Evaluate Common User Land Transport Report (CULT) for available crews	Unit LMTV MTV HEMTT M871 M872 PLS - TL 3 SUS 2 9 24 23 40 10 6 12 SUS 0 0 0 46 50 0 0 6 SUS 4 6 12 20 43 0 0			
(e) Determine which unit will provide assets (CULT reports)	Unit LMTV MTV HEMTT M871 M872 PLS - TL 3 SUS 2 9 24 23 40 10 6			
(f) Evaluate availability of Intra-theater air	No			
(g) Evaluate availability of Channel Flights (Strata-air)	No			
(4) Loading commodity				
(a) Project available staging, spotting, and loading times	090019FEB08			
(b) Available personnel	Yes			

(c) Available Material Handling Equipment (MHE), example forklifts, Rich, K-loader, etc.	Yes
Task: Conduct Resource Optimization	
(1) Review Distribution Matrixes for opportune movement for space on existing projected platforms	No
(2) Review Distribution Matrixes for opportunity to add new platforms to convoys not over the ROE limit in theater.	Convoy # origin destination add platforms 3SUS08 LSA JACKSON FOB ATLANTA 2 M872
(3) Review Distribution Matrixes for opportunity to add new platforms to convoys not over the ROE limit outside theater	Convoy # origin destination add platforms 4SUS03 LSA DALLAS FOB ATLANTA 2 M872

Staff Section: Movement Control Battalion	
Task: Evaluate Route Status	**Answers**
(1) Use Route Status (MSR/ASR) Data Information Displays	Yes
(2) Designate available route and spot time that meets TTD	Yes
Task: Availability of Force Protection platforms and security	
(1) Availability of gun trucks by location	Yes
(2) Availability of security windows	Yes
(3) MCT will notify the Transportation Company and the group providing security and designate a Spot Time that meets TTD	Yes

Integrate Plans / Organize Plans / Synchronize Plans

COA 1	
Task: Priority of Support	**Answers**
(1) Available stocks	Yes
(a) Determine number of cases	A059 - 500 boxes A131 - 200 boxes A576 - 100 boxes
(b) Determine whether there is an adequate supply of ammunition within theater	LSA JACKSON
(c) Use LOG Reporting Data Information Displays (automated or analog)	Yes

(c) Evaluate On-Hand Stock Status Reports, with no due-outs		Quantity On-hand with no Due-outs
(2) Reliable customer base		No
Task: Provide movement Platforms		
(1) Submission of Transportation Movement Request (TMR)		Yes
(2) Validation of TMR that meets timeframe		Yes
(3) Equipment		
(a) Determine transports required to make the move	A059-500 box-11pallets A131-200 box-5 pallets A576-100 box-3 pallets Total pallets= 19	2 M872 Trailer
(b) Evaluate availability of Intra-theater air		No
(c) Evaluate availability of Channel Flights (Strata-air)		No
(4) Loading commodity		
(a) Project available staging, spotting, and loading times		090019FEB08
(b) Available personnel		Yes
(c) Available Material Handling Equipment (MHE), example forklifts, Rich, K-loader, etc.		Yes
Task: Conduct Resource Optimization		
Review Distribution Matrixes for opportunity to add new platforms to convoys not over the ROE limit in theater.		Convoy # origin destination add platforms 3SUS08 LSA JACKSON FOB ATLANTA 2 M872
Task: Evaluate Route Status		
(1) Use Route Status (MSR/ASR) Data Information Displays		Yes
(2) Designate available route and spot time that meets TTD		Yes
Task: Availability of Force Protection platforms and security		
(1) Availability of gun trucks by location		Yes

(2) Availability of security windows	Yes
(3) MCT will notify the Transportation Company and the group providing security and designate a Spot Time that meets TTD	Yes

COA 2	
Task: Priority of Support	**Answers**
(1) Available stocks	Yes
(a) Determine number of cases	A059 - 500 boxes A131 - 200 boxes A576 - 100 boxes
(b) Determine whether there is an adequate supply of ammunition within theater	LSA DALLAS
(c) Use LOG Reporting Data Information Displays (automated or analog)	Yes
(d) Evaluate On-Hand Stock Status Reports, with no due-outs	Quantity On-hand with no Due-outs
(e) Support from outside theater resources	Yes (Time permit?)
(2) Reliable customer base	No
Task: Provide movement Platforms	
(1) Submission of Transportation Movement Request (TMR)	Yes
(2) Validation of TMR that meets timeframe	Yes
(3) Equipment	
(a) Determine transports required to make the move	A059-500 box- 11pallets A131-200 box- 5 pallets A576-100 box- 3 pallets Total pallets= 19	2 M872 Trailer
(b) Evaluate availability of Intra-theater air	No
(c) Evaluate availability of Channel Flights (Strata-air)	No
(4) Loading commodity	

(a) Project available staging, spotting, and loading times	090019FEB08
(b) Available personnel	Yes
(c) Available Material Handling Equipment (MHE), example forklifts, Rich, K-loader, etc.	Yes
Task: Conduct Resource Optimization	
Review Distribution Matrixes for opportunity to add new platforms to convoys not over the ROE limit outside theater	Convoy # origin destination add platforms 4SUS03 LSA DALLAS FOB ATLANTA 2 M872
Task: Evaluate Route Status	
(1) Use Route Status (MSR/ASR) Data Information Displays	Yes
(2) Designate available route and spot time that meets TTD	Yes
Task: Availability of Force Protection platforms and security	
(1) Availability of gun trucks by location	Yes
(2) Availability of security windows	Yes
(3) MCT will notify the Transportation Company and the group providing security and designate a Spot Time that meets TTD	Yes

Chapter 11

Execution

Concept

The execution of MDMP is the war-game process that displays shortfalls pertaining to recourses, as well as required coordination. Courses of Actions (COA) are tested for feasibility and productivity, and may be eliminated or revised during the war-game process. The execution process provides a capability to war-game the plan developed against different scenarios and assists in gaining insight into the decision-making processes and crisis management that exploit tangible conclusions. The scenario may not even require a conclusion; once a set number of decisions has been made and the time allotted has run out, the scenario will finish regardless of whether the original situation has been resolved or not.

Theory and Execution

Step 4: COA Analysis (War Game)

Crisis Management

COA 1	
	Answers
Task: Priority of Support	
(1) Available stocks	Yes
(a) Determine number of cases	A059 - 500 boxes A131 - 200 boxes A576 - 100 boxes
(b) Determine whether there is an adequate supply of ammunition within theater	LSA JACKSON
(c) Use LOG Reporting Data Information Displays (automated or analog)	Yes
(d) Evaluate On-Hand Stock Status Reports, with no due-outs	Quantity On-hand with no Due-outs
(2) Reliable customer base	No
Task: Provide movement Platforms	

(a) Submission of Transportation Movement Request (TMR)	Yes
(b) Validation of TMR that meets timeframe	Yes
(3) Equipment	
(a) Determine transports required to make the move — A059-500 box-<u>11pallets</u> A131-200 box-<u>5 pallets</u> A576-100 box-<u>3 pallets</u> Total pallets= 19	2 M872 Trailer
(b) Evaluate availability of Intra-theater air	No
(c) Evaluate availability of Channel Flights (Strata-air)	No
(4) Loading commodity	
(a) Project available staging, spotting, and loading times	090019FEB08
(b) Available personnel	Yes
(c) Available Material Handling Equipment (MHE), example forklifts, Rich, K-loader, etc.	Yes
Task: Conduct Resource Optimization	
(1) Review Distribution Matrixes for opportunity to add new platforms to convoys not over the ROE limit in theater.	Convoy # origin destination add platforms 3SUS08 LSA JACKSON FOB ATLANTA 2 M872
Task: Evaluate Route Status	
(1) Use Route Status (MSR/ASR) Data Information Displays	Yes
(2) Designate available route and spot time that meets TTD	Yes
Task: Availability of Force Protection platforms and security	
(1) Availability of gun trucks by Location	Yes
(2) Availability of security Windows	Yes
(3) MCT will notify the Transportation Company and	Yes

the group providing security and designate a Spot Time that meets TTD	

COA 2	
	Answers
Task: Priority of Support	
(1) Available stocks	Yes
(a) Determine number of cases	A059 - 500 boxes A131 - 200 boxes A576 - 100 boxes
(b) Determine whether there is an adequate supply of ammunition within theater	LSA DALLAS
(c) Use LOG Reporting Data Information Displays (automated or analog)	Yes
(d) Evaluate On-Hand Stock Status Reports, with no due-outs	Quantity On-hand with no Due-outs
(e) Support from outside theater resources	Yes ✓ (Time doesn't permit)
(2) Reliable customer base	No
Task: Provide movement Platforms	
(1) Submission of Transportation Movement Request (TMR)	Yes
(2) Validation of TMR that meets timeframe	Yes
(3) Equipment	
(a) Determine transports required to make the move — A059-500 box- 11pallets A131-200 box- 5 pallets A576-100 box- 3 pallets Total pallets= 19	2 M872 Trailer
(b) Evaluate availability of Intra-theater air	No
(c) Evaluate availability of Channel Flights (Strata-air)	No
(4) Loading commodity	

(a) Project available staging, spotting, and loading times	090019FEB08
(b) Available personnel	Yes
(c) Available Material Handling Equipment (MHE), example forklifts, Rich, K-loader, etc.	Yes
Task: Conduct Resource Optimization	
(1) Review Distribution Matrixes for opportunity to add new platforms to convoys not over the ROE limit outside theater	Convoy # origin destination add platforms 4SUS03 LSA DALLAS FOB ATLANTA 2 M872
Task: Evaluate Route Status	
(1) Use Route Status (MSR/ASR) Data Information Displays	Yes
(2) Designate available route and spot time that meets TTD	Yes
Task: Availability of Force Protection platforms and security	
(1) Availability of gun trucks by Location	Yes
(2) Availability of security Windows	Yes
(3) MCT will notify the Transportation Company and the group providing security and designate a Spot Time that meets TTD	Yes

Chapter 12

Analysis

Concept

The analysis function allows the capability to playback the scenarios to question-ask. The analysis process provides the user the ability to re-look critical aspects of the scenario to second-guess decision points and key movements to ask what actually happened, why it happened, and how could the plan be improved to sustain performance. The process allows the staff to make adjustments and corrections to the existing plan and resubmit the plan to the war-gaming mode or validate the plan and send to the order production phase.

Theory and Execution

Step 5: COA Comparison

Playback Mode

1. Question asking.
2. What happened?
3. Why did it happen?
4. How can one sustain performance?
5. How can one improve performance?
6. Who is responsible to ensure performance?

Results

COA 2	
(e) Support from outside theater resources	✓ (Time doesn't permit)

Step 6: COA Approval

COA 1	
	Answers
(2) Review Distribution Matrixes for opportunity to add new platforms to convoys not over the ROE limit in theater.	Convoy # origin destination add platforms 3SUS08 LSA JACKSON FOB ATLANTA 2 M872

Chapter 13

Documentation

Concept

The final requirement is the order production phase allowing the staff to produce documentation. This level also allows for sharing of database and scenario information.

Theory and Execution

Step 7: Orders Production

1. Five-Paragraph OPORD
2. Execution Matrix
3. Synchronization Matrix
4. Movement Order
5. Distribution Matrix
6. Execution Checklists
7. WARNO with the Refined COA
8. Graphics, Maps, and Diagrams
9. Share Database and Products
10. Plans

COA 1	
	Answers
Task: Priority of Support	
(1) Available stocks	Yes
(a) Determine number of cases	A059 - 500 boxes A131 - 200 boxes A576 - 100 boxes
(b) Determine whether there is an adequate supply of ammunition within theater	LSA JACKSON
(c) Use LOG Reporting Data Information Displays (automated or analog)	Yes
(d) Evaluate On-Hand Stock Status Reports, with no due-outs	Quantity On-hand with no Due-outs
(2) Reliable customer base	No

Task: Provide movement Platforms		
(a) Submission of Transportation Movement Request (TMR)		Yes
(b) Validation of TMR that meets timeframe		Yes
(3) Equipment		
(a) Determine transports required to make the move	A059-500 box-11pallets A131-200 box-5 pallets A576-100 box-3 pallets Total pallets= 19	2 M872 Trailer
(b) Evaluate availability of Intra-theater air		No
(c) Evaluate availability of Channel Flights (Strata-air)		No
(4) Loading commodity		
(a) Project available staging, spotting, and loading times		090019FEB08
(b) Available personnel		Yes
(c) Available Material Handling Equipment (MHE), example forklifts, Rich, K-loader, etc.		Yes
Task: Conduct Resource Optimization		
(3) Review Distribution Matrixes for opportunity to add new platforms to convoys not over the ROE limit in theater.		Convoy # origin destination add platforms 3SUS08 LSA JACKSON FOB ATLANTA 2 M872
Task: Evaluate Route Status		
(1) Use Route Status (MSR/ASR) Data Information Displays		Yes
(2) Designate available route and spot time that meets TTD		Yes
Task: Availability of Force Protection platforms and security		
(1) Availability of gun trucks by location		Yes
(2) Availability of security windows		Yes

(3) MCT will notify the Transportation Company and the group providing security and designate a Spot Time that meets TTD	Yes

Execution

Chapter 14

Commodity and Platform Management

Mission

The Support Operations Officer (SPO) receives a mission from higher headquarters directing resupply of ammunition (Class V) to Forward Operating Base (FOB) ATLANTA, a support base within the Brigades area of responsibility, within the next 24-hour support cycle. You are located on Logistical Support Area (LSA) JACKSON.

There are no convoys projected to go to FOB ATLANTA during that period on the Distribution. This depicts the need to schedule a new convoy. Note: air assets are not available.

Theory and Execution

This scenario focuses on Phase I of the 72-hour logistics cycle that supports the Distribution Management Process. It is designed to provide a simple single-commodity situation, which must be resolved by analyzing the mission requirements and consulting a number of different reports (LOG and CULT reports and Distribution Matrix), coordinate with supply points and movement control battalion (MCB), and ultimately construct a Transportation Movement Request (TMR).

The execution process consists of three fundamentals that provide organization to the process and these are the objectives to be accomplished, the tasks to be conducted and the ultimately the decisions that are concluded and executed (See Figure 26; Execution Process Diagram).

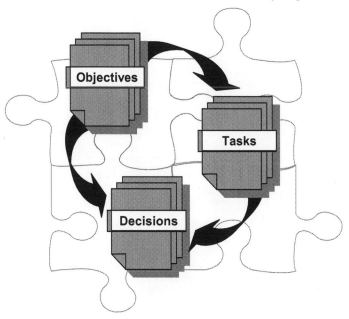

Figure 26; Execution Process Diagram

The following diagrams takes the information provided in the mission statement and shows the process a staff would go through to accomplish the assignment. The diagrams align objectives with tasks, and then to decisions, which provide organization and structure to the overall process. They also can provide templates for a unit to use in developing a desktop standard operating procedure (SOP), or a training synchronization matrix.

FRAGO:
The Support Operations Officer (SPO) receives a mission from higher headquarters directing resupply of ammunition (Class V) to Forward Operating Base (FOB) ATLANTA, a support base within the Brigades area of responsibility, within the next 24 hour support cycle . You are located on Logistical Support Area (LSA) JACKSON.

Specified Tasks (Primary Objectives)

COA
Analyze FRAGO and make Course of Action (COA) consistent with objectives and priorities

LOG Reports
Review LOG Reporting Data Information Displays

Stockage
Evaluate On-Hand Stock Status Reports

CULT
Evaluate (Common User Land Transport) CULT Report

Implied Tasks (Secondary Objectives)

COP Display
Create and use Common Operating Picture Data Information Displays

Coordination
Perform verbal or written coordination between Supply Activities and Movement Control Battalion

Clearances
Monitor and revise plans based on Road Clearance / Convoy Requests (TMRs)

Submit TMR
Validate, and/or revise existing Transportation Movement Requests

Essential Tasks (Additional Objectives)

Automation Enablers
Understand Mobile Tracking Devices capabilities and employment

Routes
Use Route Status (MSR/ASR) Data Information Displays

Tracking
Monitor and revise plans based on Convoy Operations Tracking

Closing
Understand, implement, and evaluate Open and Closing Reports

Push Matrix
Monitor and revise plans based on Movement Schedule

Figure 27; Commodity and Platform Management Objectives

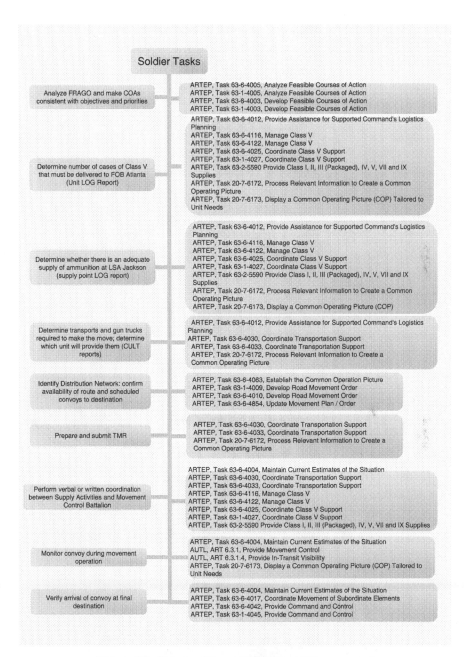

**Figure 28; Commodity and Platform Management
Soldier Tasks**

131

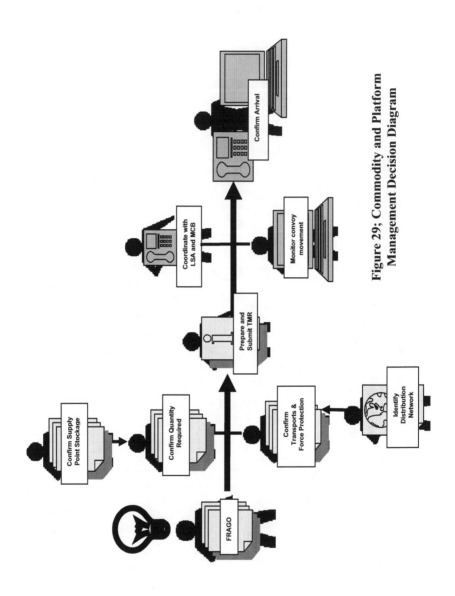

Figure 29; Commodity and Platform Management Decision Diagram

Chapter 15

Optimizing Resources

Mission

The Support Operations Officer (SPO) receives an update that A CO, 5 CAV has gone below 50% readiness for M1A1 Tanks and requires four engines within the next 24-hour resupply cycle to get them within 70% combat readiness for the next engagement. The CAV logistical support is located at Forward Operating Base (FOB) ATLANTA. You are located on Logistical Support Area (LSA) JACKSON. The Support Operations Officer (SPO) has visibility over four convoys that are projected for the next 24-hours leaving from LSA JACKSON, which provides multiple options:

(1) to create a new convoy

(2) or, to optimize projected convoy configurations

Two of the convoys the Distribution Matrix is depicting have space available to add more platforms within the maximum ROE configuration. That eliminates the need to schedule a completely new convoy. Note: air assets are not available.

Theory and Execution

The scenario focuses on Phase II of the 72-hour logistics cycle that supports the Distribution Management Process. Designed to provide a situation which must be resolved by analyzing the mission requirements and consulting a number of different reports automated and manual (LOG and CULT reports and Distribution Matrix), coordinate with supply points and movement control battalion (MCB), and ultimately construct a Transportation Movement Request (TMR) to an existing convoy. The following diagrams take you through the thought process required to accomplish the mission.

FRAGO:
The Support Operations Officer (SPO) receives an update that A CO, 5 CAV has gone below 50% readiness for M1A1 Tanks and requires four engines within the next 24-hour resupply cycle to get them within 70% combat readiness for the next engagement. The CAV logistical support is located at Forward Operating Base (FOB) Atlanta. You are located on Logistical Support Area (LSA) JACKSON. The Support Operations Officer (SPO) has visibility over four convoys that are projected for the next 24-hours leaving from LSA JACKSON.

Specified Tasks (Primary Objectives)

Implied Tasks (Secondary Objectives)

Essential Tasks (Additional Objectives)

Submit TMR
Submit/modify Transportation Movement Request for commodities and equipment

COAs
Analyze FRAGO and make COAs consistent with objectives and priorities

Automation Enablers
Understand Mobile Tracking Devices capabilities and employment

Push Matrix
Monitor and revise plans based on Movement Schedule (Push Matrix)

Coordination
Perform verbal or written coordination between Supply Activities and Movement Control Battalion

Routes
Use Route Status (MSR/ASR) Data Information Displays

CULT
Evaluate (Common User Land Transport) CULT Report

Clearances
Monitor and revise plans based on Road Clearance / Convoy Requests (TMRs)

Tracking
Monitor and revise plans based on Convoy Operations Tracking

Closing
Understand, implement, and evaluate Open and Closing Reports

Stockage
Evaluate On-Hand Stock Status Reports

Submit TMR
Validate, and/or revise existing Transportation Movement Requests

Push Matrix
Monitor and revise plans based on Movement Schedule

Figure 30; Optimizing Resources Objectives

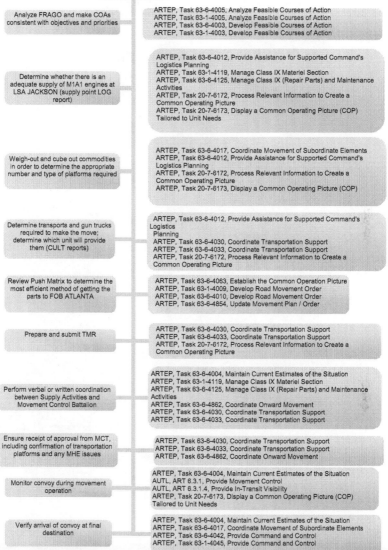

Figure 31; Optimizing Resources Soldier Tasks

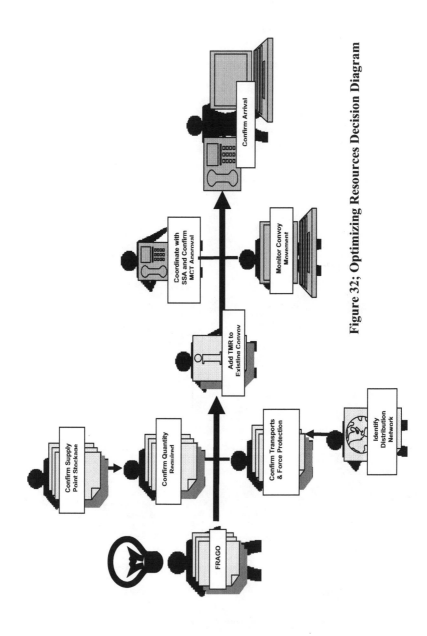

Figure 32; Optimizing Resources Decision Diagram

Chapter 16

Redistribution

Mission

The Support Operations Officer (SPO) receives an update that 5 CAV, a unit at FOB ATLANTA is preparing for a future operation and has requested 350,000 gallons of JP8 fuel to be delivered the next support cycle. Shortly after the convoys arrive to deliver the fuel, the SPO receives a message advising that the unit had requested too much fuel in advance of the operation, and the FOB does not have sufficient storage capacity for all the fuel that was delivered. Unit commander wants to hold on to the fuel tankers. The tankers could be there for two to three days before there is adequate storage capacity for the remaining fuel. Leaving the tankers there could significantly affect the SPO sustainment cycles over the next three days, as well as support to future missions, which provides multiple options:

1. Approve leaving the tankers at the FOB ATLANTA until there is adequate storage capacity for the remaining fuel

2. Backhaul the excess fuel back to original location

3. Send the remaining fuel to a different location to support other sustainment cycle requirements.

Theory and Execution

The scenario also focuses on Phase II of the 72-hour logistics cycle. The staff must analyze the mission requirements and consult a number of different reports automated and manual (LOG and CULT reports and Distribution Matrix), coordinate with supply points and movement control battalion (MCB), and ultimately construct a Transportation Movement Request (TMR) to an existing convoy. Backhaul to me is not a very good option, in this case. It is not being productive with resources and future requirement, but option 3 is a good choice supporting the concept of redistribution. The following diagrams take you through the thought process required to accomplish the mission.

FRAGO:
The Support Operations Officer (SPO) receives an update that 5 CAV, a unit at FOB ATLANTA is preparing for a future operation and has requested 350,000 gallons of JP8 fuel be delivered the next support cycle. Shortly after the convoys arrive to deliver the fuel, the SPO receives a message advising that the unit had requested too much fuel in advance of the operation, and the FOB does not have sufficient storage capacity for all the fuel

Specified Tasks (Primary Objectives)	Implied Tasks (Secondary Objectives)	Essential Tasks (Additional Objectives)
COA Analyze FRAGO and make Course of Action (COA) consistent with objectives and priorities	**COP Display** Create and use Common Operating Picture Data Information Displays	**Automation Enablers** Understand Mobile Tracking Devices capabilities and employment
LOG Reports Review Unit and Supply Point LOG Reporting Data Information Displays	**Coordination** Perform verbal or written coordination between Supply Activities and Movement Control Battalion	**Routes** Use Route Status (MSR/ASR) Data Information Displays
Stockage Evaluate On-Hand Stock Status and Storage Capacity Reports	**Clearances** Monitor and revise plans based on Road Clearance / Convoy Requests (TMRs)	**Tracking** Monitor and revise plans based on Convoy Operations Tracking
CULT Evaluate (Common User Land Transport) CULT Report for Force Protection Assets	**Submit TMR** Submit Onward Movement Validate Transportation Movement Requests	**Closing** Understand, implement, and evaluate Open and Closing Reports
		Push Matrix Monitor and revise plans based on Movement Schedule

Figure 33; Redistribution Objectives

Figure 34; Redistribution Soldier Tasks

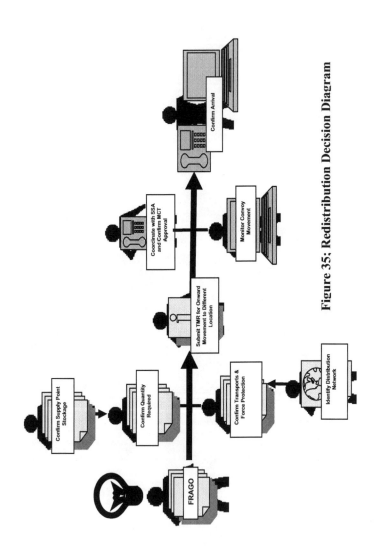

Figure 35: Redistribution Decision Diagram

Chapter 17

Lateral Distribution

Mission

The Support Operations Officer (SPO) receives a mission from higher headquarters directing an emergency resupply of Class III Bulk to Forward Operating Base (FOB) ATLANTA. One of the convoys being tracked has the sufficient gallons of Class III Bulk that could be diverted to FOB ATLANTA.

There are no convoys projected to go to FOB ATLANTA during that period on the Distribution Matrix. No assets are available until 48-hours, and air assets are not available.

Theory and Execution

The scenario focuses on Phase IV (Tracking) of the 72-hour logistics cycle, and one of my own theories called lateral Distribution. The staff analyzes the mission requirements and consults different automated and manual reports (LOG and CULT reports and Distribution Matrix), and coordinates with movement control battalion (MCB to redirect convoy to alternate location. The following diagrams take you through the thought process required to accomplish the mission.

FRAGO:
The Support Operations Officer (SPO) receives a mission from higher headquarters directing an emergency resupply of Class III Bulk to Forward Operating Base (FOB) ATLANTA. One of the convoys being track has the sufficient gallons of Class III Bulk that could be diverted to FOB ATLANTA. There are no convoys projected to go to FOB ATLANTA during that period on the Distribution Matrix. No assets are available until 48-hours. and air assets are not available.

Specified Tasks (Primary Objectives)

COA
Analyze FRAGO and make Course of Action (COA) consistent with objectives and priorities

LOG Reports
Review Unit and Supply Point LOG Reporting Data Information Displays

Stockage
Evaluate On-Hand Stock Status and Storage Capacity Reports

CULT
Evaluate (Common User Land Transport) CULT Report for Force Protection Assets

Push Matrix
Monitor and revise plans based on Movement Schedule

Implied Tasks (Secondary Objectives)

COP Display
Create and use Common Operating Picture Data Information Displays

Coordination
Perform verbal or automated coordination between Convoy and Movement Control Teams

Clearances
Monitor and revise plans based on Road Clearance / Convoy Requests (TMRs)

Submit TMR
Submit Onward Movement Validate Transportation Movement Requests

Essential Tasks (Additional Objectives)

Automation Enablers
Understand Mobile Tracking Devices capabilities and employment

Routes
Use Route Status (MSR/ASR) Data Information Displays

Tracking
Monitor and revise plans based on Convoy Operations Tracking

Closing
Understand, implement, and evaluate Open and Closing Reports

Figure 36; Lateral Distribution Objectives

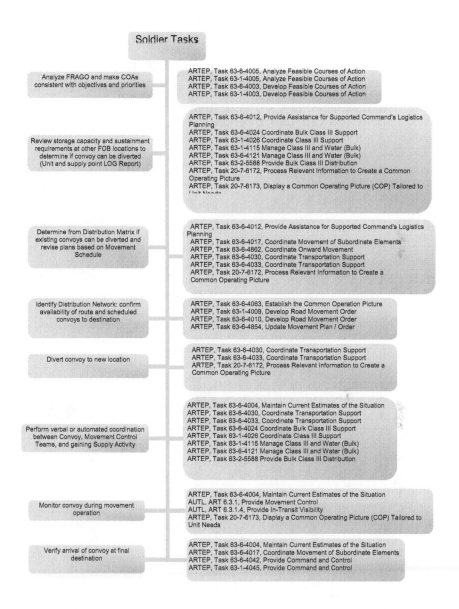

Soldier Tasks

Analyze FRAGO and make COAs consistent with objectives and priorities	ARTEP, Task 63-6-4005, Analyze Feasible Courses of Action ARTEP, Task 63-1-4005, Analyze Feasible Courses of Action ARTEP, Task 63-6-4003, Develop Feasible Courses of Action ARTEP, Task 63-1-4003, Develop Feasible Courses of Action
Review storage capacity and sustainment requirements at other FOB locations to determine if convoy can be diverted (Unit and supply point LOG Report)	ARTEP, Task 63-6-4012, Provide Assistance for Supported Command's Logistics Planning ARTEP, Task 63-6-4024 Coordinate Bulk Class III Support ARTEP, Task 63-1-4026 Coordinate Class III Support ARTEP, Task 63-1-4115 Manage Class III and Water (Bulk) ARTEP, Task 63-6-4121 Manage Class III and Water (Bulk) ARTEP, Task 63-2-5588 Provide Bulk Class III Distribution ARTEP, Task 20-7-6172, Process Relevant Information to Create a Common Operating Picture ARTEP, Task 20-7-6173, Display a Common Operating Picture (COP) Tailored to Unit Needs
Determine from Distribution Matrix if existing convoys can be diverted and revise plans based on Movement Schedule	ARTEP, Task 63-6-4012, Provide Assistance for Supported Command's Logistics Planning ARTEP, Task 63-6-4017, Coordinate Movement of Subordinate Elements ARTEP, Task 63-6-4862, Coordinate Onward Movement ARTEP, Task 63-6-4030, Coordinate Transportation Support ARTEP, Task 63-6-4033, Coordinate Transportation Support ARTEP, Task 20-7-6172, Process Relevant Information to Create a Common Operating Picture
Identify Distribution Network: confirm availability of route and scheduled convoys to destination	ARTEP, Task 63-6-4063, Establish the Common Operation Picture ARTEP, Task 63-1-4009, Develop Road Movement Order ARTEP, Task 63-6-4010, Develop Road Movement Order ARTEP, Task 63-6-4854, Update Movement Plan / Order
Divert convoy to new location	ARTEP, Task 63-6-4030, Coordinate Transportation Support ARTEP, Task 63-6-4033, Coordinate Transportation Support ARTEP, Task 20-7-6172, Process Relevant Information to Create a Common Operating Picture
Perform verbal or automated coordination between Convoy, Movement Control Teams, and gaining Supply Activity	ARTEP, Task 63-6-4004, Maintain Current Estimates of the Situation ARTEP, Task 63-6-4030, Coordinate Transportation Support ARTEP, Task 63-6-4033, Coordinate Transportation Support ARTEP, Task 63-6-4024 Coordinate Bulk Class III Support ARTEP, Task 63-1-4026 Coordinate Class III Support ARTEP, Task 63-1-4115 Manage Class III and Water (Bulk) ARTEP, Task 63-6-4121 Manage Class III and Water (Bulk) ARTEP, Task 63-2-5588 Provide Bulk Class III Distribution
Monitor convoy during movement operation	ARTEP, Task 63-6-4004, Maintain Current Estimates of the Situation AUTL, ART 6.3.1, Provide Movement Control AUTL, ART 6.3.1.4, Provide In-Transit Visibility ARTEP, Task 20-7-6173, Display a Common Operating Picture (COP) Tailored to Unit Needs
Verify arrival of convoy at final destination	ARTEP, Task 63-6-4004, Maintain Current Estimates of the Situation ARTEP, Task 63-6-4017, Coordinate Movement of Subordinate Elements ARTEP, Task 63-6-4042, Provide Command and Control ARTEP, Task 63-1-4045, Provide Command and Control

Figure 37; Lateral Distribution Soldier Tasks

143

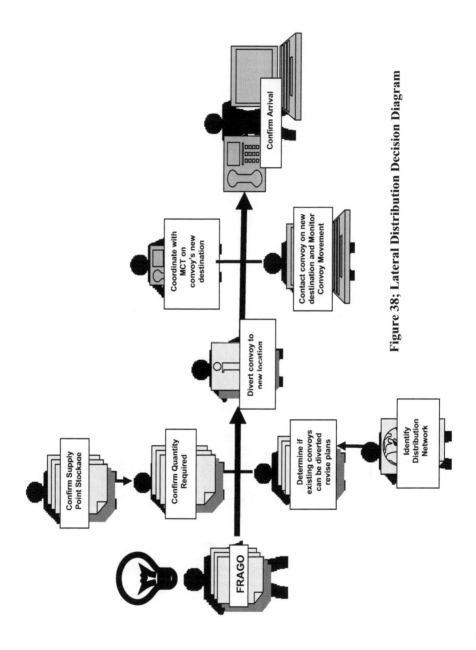

Figure 38; Lateral Distribution Decision Diagram

Staff Directed Lateral Distribution

Directed Lateral Distribution is the movement of commodities supporting high priority demands for theater operations. The process attempts to resolve commodity shortfalls through re-direction of theater stocks. Lateral

Distribution supports the commander's priorities by identifying assets to accommodate known and anticipated requirements. Asset managers retain commodity visibility and direct the lateral distribution of supplies, equipment and capabilities in support of command requirements.

The procedure consists of asset visibility forward, enabling the Distribution Management Center to redirect supplies from one transit node to another, facilitating a "Quick-Fix", until scheduled logistic pushes can arrive, and adjustments to forecasting requirements can be made.

The keys to this procedure are visibility, control and capability to adjust configured loads and redirect the flow of supplies and materiel, within the distribution networks, to provide the right resources at the right place and time to meet the commander's intent. Procedure revolves around commodity management and the staff's ability to manipulate the supply pipeline by changing or adjusting its flow. This is accomplished by either redirecting the flow in route or by altering the distribution push cycle in support of existing requirements. Bottom line - if the commodity manager has the visibility of the pipeline flow, the capability within the time, distance, and space of the distribution network to manipulate the flow and the transportation manager has the control over the transportation platforms within the distribution network to direct or redirect its movement, then staff lateral distribution can transpire. To accomplish this procedure, it takes managers (commodity and movement) that understand the theater consumption rates, the distribution push cycle established in support, platform rotation that determines availability, the transportation nodes (MCB, MCT, HRT) capacity over the network and adjustments to forecasting requirements are made. To say this is a more a supply action than transportation is immaterial. The two actions are equal in the success of the procedure. The supply manager must have visibility of the commodities under their control and the capability to change or adjust the flow in support of the Black, Red, Amber, and Green percentage rates used by the Distribution Management Center in the administration of the theater logistics. Equally important is the transportation manger's ability to have the visibility, capability and control over the movement of the distribution network to direct or redirect the flow in support of the commodity manager's intent. To achieve the required results, the most important element of the procedure has to be completed and that is the adjustment of element of the procedure has to be completed and that is the adjustment of the region forecast, as well as the distribution push cycle to replace the diverted commodities. This can be attained by either adding additional platforms, adjusting existing convoy rotations over a set period utilizing contingency stocks.

(Elements Influencing)   **(Actions Influencing)**

Visibility, Capability, Control + **Changing or Adjustment**   = **Staff Lateral Distribution**
           Pipeline Flow   **Forecast / Distribution Push Cycle**

Chapter 18

Reception, Staging, and Onward Movement

Mission

The Brigade Commander needs a daily update of the status of personnel and equipment flowing from CONUS to the theater. During the course of tracking equipment, the SPO discovers that the unit has lost visibility over some items of equipment and some items have been misrouted. The task is to find the equipment, for those that have been misrouted identify their current locations, and submit TMRs to re-route the equipment to the proper location.

Theory and Execution

The scenario focuses on the strategic level of movement into theater and encompasses Phase I (144+-hours) to the unit's reception in theater, then the units staging process Phase II (120-hours), and ultimately the unit's onward movement Phases III and IV (96-84 hours) deployment cycle. The staff must analyze the mission requirements and consult a number of different reports (Movement Tables (Schedule), CULT reports, and Distribution Matrix), and different automated systems (BCS3, ITV, TC-AIMS II block 2 and 3, WPS and GATES). They need to coordinate with port movement control teams (MCT) and movement control battalion (MCB), and ultimately create Transportation Movement Requests (TMRs) to re-route lost equipment to the proper unit tactical assemble area (TAA). The staff must understand that the new capability that In-Transit Visibility (ITV) provides the unit in tracking and identifying lost or misrouted equipment during the deployment process. Some of the new automation systems and tracking devices available to the unit to date are Radio Frequency Identification Devises (RFID) tags, fixed interrogators, and mobile tracking device. As long as the unit manifests their Deployment Equipment Lists (DEL) to level six data fidelity, the equipment and personnel can be tracked en-route utilizing BCS3 or the information of last known location can be identified and tracked using other ITV systems (BCS3, ITV, TC-AIMS II block 2 and 3, WPS and GATES). The staff's major objective is to conduct the research aimed at providing a timely status update for the commander regarding the transport of unit personnel and equipment to the theater. To accomplish the objective there are a series of tasks that the staff must understand consisting of: Reception,

Staging, and Onward Movement (RSO) concepts, including specific personnel tasks. Also, be able to analysis, examine, and create plans based on air and sea ports of debarkation (SPOD and APOD) interrogator information. Lastly, to know how to create and evaluate displays from the Common Operating Picture Data using the different automated systems. The following diagrams take you through the thought process required to accomplish the mission.

Figure 39; Reception, Staging, and Onward Movement (RSO) Concept

FRAGO:
The Brigade Commander wants a daily update of the status of personnel and equipment flowing from CONUS to the theater. During the course of tracking equipment, the SPO discovers that the unit has lost visibility over some items of equipment and some items have been misrouted. The task is to find the equipment, for those that have been misrouted identify locations, and submit TMRs to re-route the equipment to the proper location.

Specified Tasks (Primary Objectives)	Implied Tasks (Secondary Objectives)	Essential Tasks (Additional Objectives)
COA Analyze FRAGO and make Course of Action (COA) consistent with objectives and priorities	**COP Display** Create and use Common Operating Picture Data Information Displays	**Automation Enablers** Understand Mobile Tracking Devices capabilities and employment
Analysis Conduct research and determine the status of personnel and equipment flowing from CONUS to the theater	**Coordination** Perform verbal or written coordination between Supply Activities, Movement Control Teams, and Movement Control Battalion	**Routes** Use Route Status (MSR/ASR) Data Information Displays
Locate Find equipment that is either missing or unaccounted	**Clearances** Monitor and revise plans based on Road Clearance / Convoy Requests (TMRs)	**Tracking** Monitor and revise plans based on Convoy Operations Tracking
Planning & Preparation Develop plan to re-route misrouted equipment to the proper location	**Submit TMR** Submit Onward Movement Validate Transportation Movement Requests	**Push Matrix** Monitor and revise plans based on Movement Schedule
		Receiving Understand, implement, and evaluate Open and Closing Reports

Figure 40; Reception, Staging, and Onward Movement Objectives

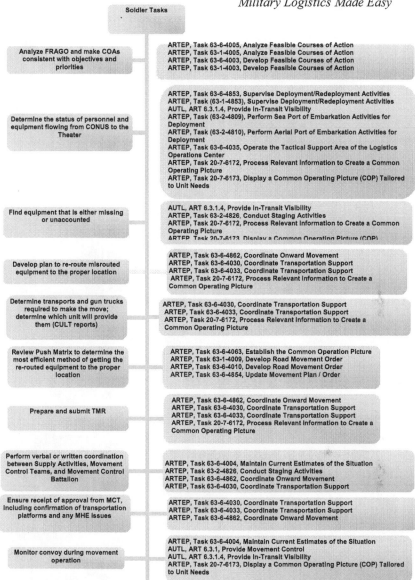

Soldier Tasks

| Analyze FRAGO and make COAs consistent with objectives and priorities | ARTEP, Task 63-6-4005, Analyze Feasible Courses of Action
ARTEP, Task 63-1-4005, Analyze Feasible Courses of Action
ARTEP, Task 63-6-4003, Develop Feasible Courses of Action
ARTEP, Task 63-1-4003, Develop Feasible Courses of Action |

Determine the status of personnel and equipment flowing from CONUS to the Theater
ARTEP, Task 63-6-4853, Supervise Deployment/Redeployment Activities
ARTEP, Task (63-1-4853), Supervise Deployment/Redeployment Activities
AUTL, ART 6.3.1.4, Provide In-Transit Visibility
ARTEP, Task (63-2-4809), Perform Sea Port of Embarkation Activities for Deployment
ARTEP, Task (63-2-4810), Perform Aerial Port of Embarkation Activities for Deployment
ARTEP, Task 63-6-4035, Operate the Tactical Support Area of the Logistics Operations Center
ARTEP, Task 20-7-6172, Process Relevant Information to Create a Common Operating Picture
ARTEP, Task 20-7-6173, Display a Common Operating Picture (COP) Tailored to Unit Needs

Find equipment that is either missing or unaccounted
AUTL, ART 6.3.1.4, Provide In-Transit Visibility
ARTEP, Task 63-2-4826, Conduct Staging Activities
ARTEP, Task 20-7-6172, Process Relevant Information to Create a Common Operating Picture
ARTEP, Task 20-7-6173, Display a Common Operating Picture (COP)

Develop plan to re-route misrouted equipment to the proper location
ARTEP, Task 63-6-4862, Coordinate Onward Movement
ARTEP, Task 63-6-4030, Coordinate Transportation Support
ARTEP, Task 63-6-4033, Coordinate Transportation Support
ARTEP, Task 20-7-6172, Process Relevant Information to Create a Common Operating Picture

Determine transports and gun trucks required to make the move; determine which unit will provide them (CULT reports)
ARTEP, Task 63-6-4030, Coordinate Transportation Support
ARTEP, Task 63-6-4033, Coordinate Transportation Support
ARTEP, Task 20-7-6172, Process Relevant Information to Create a Common Operating Picture

Review Push Matrix to determine the most efficient method of getting the re-routed equipment to the proper location
ARTEP, Task 63-6-4063, Establish the Common Operation Picture
ARTEP, Task 63-1-4009, Develop Road Movement Order
ARTEP, Task 63-6-4010, Develop Road Movement Order
ARTEP, Task 63-6-4854, Update Movement Plan / Order

Prepare and submit TMR
ARTEP, Task 63-6-4862, Coordinate Onward Movement
ARTEP, Task 63-6-4030, Coordinate Transportation Support
ARTEP, Task 63-6-4033, Coordinate Transportation Support
ARTEP, Task 20-7-6172, Process Relevant Information to Create a Common Operating Picture

Perform verbal or written coordination between Supply Activities, Movement Control Teams, and Movement Control Battalion
ARTEP, Task 63-6-4004, Maintain Current Estimates of the Situation
ARTEP, Task 63-2-4826, Conduct Staging Activities
ARTEP, Task 63-6-4862, Coordinate Onward Movement
ARTEP, Task 63-6-4030, Coordinate Transportation Support

Ensure receipt of approval from MCT, including confirmation of transportation platforms and any MHE issues
ARTEP, Task 63-6-4030, Coordinate Transportation Support
ARTEP, Task 63-6-4033, Coordinate Transportation Support
ARTEP, Task 63-6-4862, Coordinate Onward Movement

Monitor convoy during movement operation
ARTEP, Task 63-6-4004, Maintain Current Estimates of the Situation
AUTL, ART 6.3.1, Provide Movement Control
AUTL, ART 6.3.1.4, Provide In-Transit Visibility
ARTEP, Task 20-7-6173, Display a Common Operating Picture (COP) Tailored to Unit Needs

Verify arrival of convoy at final destination
ARTEP, Task 63-6-4004, Maintain Current Estimates of the Situation
ARTEP, Task 63-2-4813, Prepare Equipment Reception Team for Tactical Road March ARTEP, Task 63-6-4042, Provide Command and Control
ARTEP, Task 63-1-4045, Provide Command and Control

Figure 41; Reception, Staging, and Onward Movement Soldier Tasks

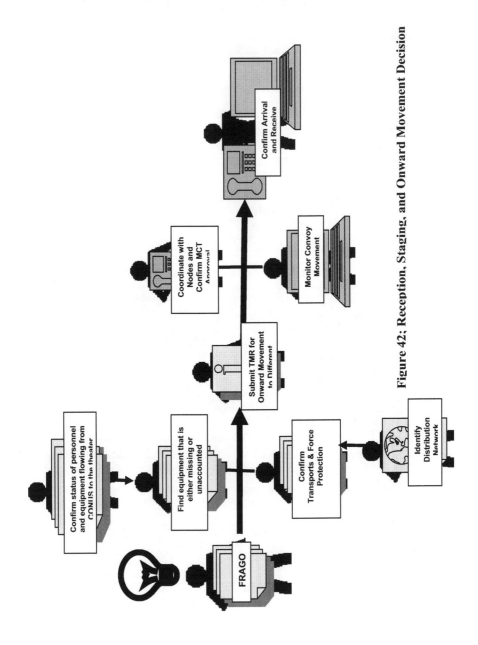

Figure 42: Reception, Staging, and Onward Movement Decision

Reception, Staging, Onward Movement, and
Integration (RSO&I)

The key to tracking Combat Power during deployment operations is to develop a process which links automated tracking capabilities with physical movement requirements. The automations system that is best suited for tracking air, ground, and sea movement is the Battle Command Sustainment Support System (BCS3). BCS3 has the capability to track planes, vehicles, trains and ships as long as there is a mobile interrogator device attached to the mode of transportation. BCS3 can also track Radio Frequency Identification Devices (RFID) tags by utilizing fixed interrogator devices located along the route of embarkation (Distribution Network) that identifies its last known location. If the RFID tag signal is strong enough, you can sometimes track an individual tag, but this is not a recommended procedure due to its limited ability to produce a strong and constant signal. There are certain required steps that units must adhere for them to be successful in tracking combat power arriving into the theater of operation. To have success in tracking RSO&I with BCS3, there are five steps in the process that a unit needs to conduct; (1) Plan (2) Manifest (3) Schedule (4) Track and (5) Receive. The following provides a detailed description of each step:

Step One: Identify the Distribution Network (***Plan***).
Review the area of operation to identify key nodes, road networks, air and fixed interrogator capability within the distribution network established at the time of deployment. Due to combat operations, the unit may be limited in physical assets available for deployment support, but with prior planning, a unit can make an immature infrastructure work to their advantage. Also, with adequate planning, a unit could make additional improvements to the distribution network infrastructure before the main deployment assets arrive. An example would be to place additional interrogator devices at port and air facilities and/or along the route to the tactical assemble area (TAA).

Step Two: Create Deployment Equipment Lists (DEL) to level six data fidelity (***Manifest***). The most important part of any distribution operation, whether it is a deployment, redeployment, rest of troops or sustainment operations, is a complete and detailed manifest of commodities and contents of the containers or equipment to be shipped. These manifests should be populated to Radio Frequency Identification Devises (RFID) tags and attached to each load for identification along the route of movement. Problems with not creating a detailed manifest include looking for a certain item loaded in a container, the RFID tags are only populated with the word "Container", and you have one hundred containers. If you are lucky, you will pick the right one - if not, you will open all one hundred containers before you find the item you require. When the RFID tag contains detailed content data, a unit can review the container manifest within BCS3 and retain the container number of the container holding the required item. Remember, the key to a successful RSO&I, is smooth and swift integration of personnel, equipment and commodities within the theater of operation.

Step Three: Identify mode of transportation and establish Movement Tables (*Schedule*). Creating movement plans that identify loads with transportation platforms to link the type of mobile integration device utilized for tracking movement is a combination of air, sea and ground. This movement table organizes the manifest to movement lifts and convoys, providing a distribution matrix that can be used to identify what lifts and convoys need to be tracked, when and how often in BCS3. An example - if a unit is leaving Fort Hood, Texas, by rail and deploying to the National Training Center (NTC), CA, and you know it will take three days for the equipment and commodities to arrive at the staging area; do you need to track the train? The answer is "No", if you are not going to do anything with the equipment or commodity until it arrives at the staging area. Only then do you need BCS3 to tell you if it does not pass the fix integrators at the staging area on the third day. The time to track the equipment and commodities in BCS3 is its onward movement through the desert to the dust bowl at NTC proper. This movement schedule can depict key muscle movements for the unit to conduct in the area of monitoring or actively tracking the equipment or commodities in BCS3.

Step Four: Synchronize and link automated tracking capabilities, with mode of transportation, throughout the route of movement (*Track*). By utilizing the movement table, which identifies the mode of transportation and its mobile interrogator device or RFID tag numbers, the unit can decide the lifts and convoys that need to be tracked within BCS3. The unit can track the lift or convoy as a virtual movement when the schedule identifies the manifest with the mobile tracking interrogator device and mounts the manifests to the mobile interrogator device icon in BCS3. If the schedule shows that the commodity is to be tracked by RFID tags, then the fixed interrogators located along the route of movement are identified and proximity alerts are created within BCS3 to display as the fix interrogators identify the tags.

Step Five: Process commodities as they arrive in theater (*Receive*). Process and receive equipment and commodities to reflect combat power build-up, and to assist unit with onward movement and integration within theater of operation. By having BCS3 track or alert the unit as critical equipment or commodities arrive at the port of embarkation, the unit can anticipate onward movement to unit tactical assembly areas and request for drives by type and proper numbers to match with onward movement convoy schedules previously talked about above. This can eliminate movement delays and facilitate a smooth integration within theater for units to meet, train-up and rehearse requirements.

In conclusion - a unit that pays attention to detail and ensures that all equipment and commodities are properly manifested with content data fidelity, conducts prior planning and scheduling, and utilizes new automation systems and tracking devices, then this unit can eliminate movement delays and facilitate a smooth integration within theater for units to meet, train-up and rehearse requirements.

Chapter 19

Tracking

Mission

The Support Operations Officer (SPO) task is to track convoys of interest, to the command, in the next 24-hour movement cycle. These convoys consist of sustainment, deployment, redeployment, reset, and other type movements. There are two 12-hour push rotations within the 24-hour cycle. SPO is interested in 25 movements for completion or forward progress. A TOC can only visually track so many convoys, so a combination of tracking methods is required (MTS, RIFD, and Proximity Alerts).

Theory and Execution

The scenario focuses on Phase IV (Tracking) of the 84-hour or 72-hour distribution cycle, depending on which level of logistical support you are conducting. The staff analyzes the mission requirements and consults different automated tracking capabilities and systems. The three major ways to track convoys, commodities, and display movement or information within the automated systems Common Operating Picture (COP) is to utilize either mobile tracking systems (MTS), combination of Radio Frequency Information Devises and Interrogators, or proximity alerts. Mobile Tracking Systems (MTS) are the preferred way to track convoy movement. It provides the capability for tracking vehicles and communicating during movement. These devices, called transponders, utilize a procedure consisting of mobile satellite two-way messaging that is wireless and flows from the tracking equipped vehicle to the control station. The second way is utilizing Radio Frequency Identification Devises (RFID), which are small electronic pieces of equipment that reflect and modify received radio wave signals. The Interrogators are electronic devices that provide radio wave frequency interface between an antenna, the RFID tag, and a computer system; this is the preferred method of tracking commodities. The last way is using proximity alerts, which is simply associating an MTS to a GEO location on the automated systems map, or RIFD tags to an interrogator so as the device passes the location or interrogator a message appears on the automated control systems screen. This is the go method of identifying, progress or choke points along the convoy route, as well as opening and closing of movement. All the above ways have their place, but the best way to implement in-transit visibility for convoy tracking is to link the vehicles in any particular movement to a mobile tracking system or transponder, this process is called creating a virtual convoy. The convoy is scheduled on a movement table, which has all the data required to identify the number of vehicles and the manifests of commodity or equipment hauled. Once this is done the organization can track the lift or convoy as a virtual movement, already having the schedule identifying the manifested items to be hauled, and the convoy and its vehicles being tracked with the mobile tracking device. The contents of the convoy can have the manifests mounted to the mobile tracking device icon depicted on the graphical map of the computer system. The following diagrams take you through the thought process required to accomplish the mission.

Concept of Tracking Ground Convoys

Proximity Alerts

- Associate an MTS device to a GEO location on BCS3 automated map display, and as device sends signal and passes location an alert screen appears on BCS3
- Associate an RFID tag to an interrogator and attach to a GEO location on BCS3 automated map display, and as RFID tag passes the location and the interrogator sends a signal an alert screen appears on BCS3
- Proximity Alerts are used to identify a convoy location, or display that a convoy passed a particular GEO location or choke point on convoy route
- To provide a positive inbound clearance report (PIC)
- Assist in convoy starting and closing times

RFID/Interrogators

- Radio Frequency Identification (RFID) system are small electronic pieces of equipment that reflect and modify received continuous radio wave signals
- The Radio Frequency modules also read and amplify returned signals prior to relaying them to a reader
- Tags are not transmitters and do not radiate signals by themselves, but are either battery powered or have intermittent generator power, and will not send back an identification signal unless interrogated by a Reader
- There are two basic types of RFID tags, active tags have an incorporated power supply or battery, and passive tags have no power supply
- Interrogators are electronic devices that provide radio wave frequency interface between an antenna, the RFID tag, and a computer system
- They generate radio frequencies, which in the case of passive tags powers the tag, through an antenna that sends and receives data from the RFID tag
- Device has a processor for managing the incoming data received from the tag, and then transmits information to the tag
- Data received from the tag is encrypted and sent to the computer system for processing

Mobile Tracking Systems

- Utilizing a procedure consisting of mobile satellite two-way messaging that is wireless and flows from the tracking equipped vehicle to the control station
- System is mounted on the vehicle and the control station component stays in communication within a prescribed timeframe to monitor vehicle locations giving near-real time tracking potential
- Communication capability between the vehicle and control station requires a commercial satellite vendor that allows components to send and receive traffic
- This type of technology allows the transportation coordinator to communicate with the operator of any vehicle, regardless of location
- New development integrates radio frequency technology and mobile tracking devices to provide the capability to read RFID tags loaded on the vehicle using the vehicle mounted transponder to support in-transit visibility

Figure 43; Tracking Ground Convoys Concept

Mission:
The Support Operations Officer (SPO) task is to track convoys of interest, to the command, in the next 24-hour movement cycle. These convoys consist of sustainment, deployment, redeployment, reset, and other type movements. There are two 12-hour push rotations within the 24-hour cycle. SPO is interested in 25 movements for completion or forward progress. A TOC can only visually track so many convoys, so a combination of tracking methods is required (MTS, RIFD, and Proximity Alerts).

Specified Tasks (Primary Objectives)

COA
Analyze FRAGO and make Course of Action (COA) consistent with objectives and priorities

Analysis
Monitor and revise plans based on Movement Schedule (Distribution Matrix, a.k.a. Push Matrix)

Confirm Movement
Monitor and revise plans based on Road Clearance/Convoy Requests (TMRs)

Tracking
Create Op-Views and Monitor Convoy Operations Movement (Mobile Tracking Systems)

Tracking
Create Op-Views and Monitor Convoy Operations Movement based on Proximity Alerts (RFID & Interrogators)

Implied Tasks (Secondary Objectives)

COP Display
Create and use Common Operating Picture Data Information Displays pertaining to ITV

Automation Enablers
Understand Mobile Tracking Systems, RFID devices, and Interrogators capabilities and employment

Clearances
Monitor and revise plans based on Road Clearance / Convoy Requests (TMRs)

Communication
Monitor Transponder Messaging Traffic capability for SPOT reports (including Panic Messages)

Essential Tasks (Additional Objectives)

Battle Drills
Implement TOC convoy emergency procedures

Routes
Use Route Status (MSR/ASR) Data Information Displays

Push Matrix
Monitor and revise plans based on Movement Schedule

Receiving
Understand, implement, and evaluate Open and Closing Reports

Submit TMR
Re-submit Onward Movement TMR for Rest Over Night (RON) convoys

Figure 44; Tracking Objectives

Figure 45; Tracking Soldier Tasks

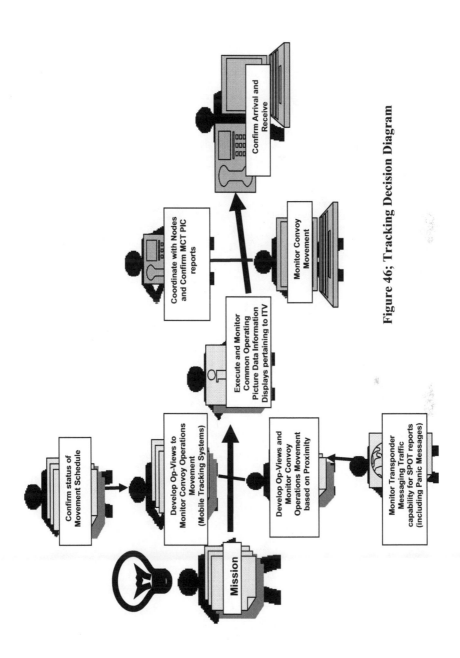

Figure 46; Tracking Decision Diagram

Situational Awareness

Chapter 20

Operational Control

Concept

The term Logistical Common Operating Picture (COP) is a template of information that links mission priorities; operational status; intelligence situation; environmental conditions; concept of support; time phased requirements; support systems and customer requirements and constraints to provide situational awareness that is common to all levels up the chain (CO, BN, BDE, GRP, CORPS, and THEATER). The concept fuses Logistical information from the supply (national and retail), maintenance (Tactical, Sustainment and Depot), and transportation (Air and Sea Ports of Embarkation/Deprecation, and convoy movements) to facilitate current and future forecasting requirements, on-hand theater inventories, in-transit visibility, customer returns (retrogrades) and repaired dues-in from maintenance. Template information assists the individual in correlating common information and channel analysis as the different layers are identified and analyzed.

Issues and solutions surface and formulate a plan or strategy of operation. All this data applies to the template for utilization at all levels, providing synergy.

Theory and Execution

The development of the computer and satellite communication has not only changed civilian business world, it has also had a major impact on today's modern battlefield. The requirement for information situational awareness is as important to the commander in the field as it is to a CEO of industry. FM 3-0, Operations, Chapter 1-37, The Information Dimension, expresses the belief that; "All military operations take place within an information environment that is largely outside the control of military forces. The information environment is the aggregate of individuals, organizations, and systems that collect, process, store, display, and disseminate information; also included is the information itself (see JP 3-13; FM 3-13). National, international, and non-state actors use this environment to collect process and disseminate information. The media's use of real-time technology affects public opinion, both in the US and abroad, and alters the conduct and perceived legitimacy of military operations. Now, more than ever, every soldier represents America— potentially to a global audience."[14]

The information-based cycle is clearly today's Army Transformation and the Distribution Management (DM) Process on which it is based. Army Transformation and the DM Process works on information superiority, enabling staffs to collect and process data that provides the commander with opinions. FM 3-0, Operations, Chapter 1-38, "The Information Dimension provides a good description of information superiority. Information superiority enables Army forces to see first, understand the situation more quickly and accurately, and act faster than their adversaries. Derived from the effective synchronization of intelligence, surveillance and reconnaissance (ISR), information management (IM), and information operations (IO) information superiority is an operational advantage that results in friendly forces gaining and retaining the initiative. Effective ISR operations and IM identify the information commanders require, collect it, and get it to them when they need it. Offensive IO degrades an adversary's will to resist and ability to fight while simultaneously denying him relevant friendly force information. Defensive information operations (IO) protect friendly information and command and control (C2) systems. Information superiority means commanders receive accurate, timely information that enables them to make better decisions and act faster than their adversaries. Early attainment of information superiority influences all aspects of Army force operations. For example, sharing accurate and current information between initial-entry and follow-on forces creates the conditions for rapid transition from deployment to employment. Sharing real-time changes in the situation among all elements of a force in contact facilitates synchronization and encourages subordinates to exercise initiative." [15] The Distribution Management Process establishes a battle rhythm for commodity and movement control centered on the logistical Common Operating Picture (COP), consisting of information management and operations relating to support, movement and force protection. The three are linked with in-transit visibility assets to improve force tracking, support distribution and provide information that is common to all levels up and down the chain (Company, Battalion, Brigade or Group, Corps, and Theater). FM 3-0, Operations, Chapter 4-29,

Information, states; "The common operational picture (COP) based on enhanced intelligence, surveillance, and reconnaissance (ISR) and disseminated by modern information systems provides commanders

---

[14] FM 3-0 (formerly FM 100-5), *Operations.* 14 June 2001, 1-37.
[15] Ibid, 1-38.

throughout the force with an accurate, near real-time perspective and knowledge of the situation,"[16] and Chapter 12-10, Combat Service Support (CSS) Planning, says; "Force commanders integrate operational and CSS planning through the Common Operating Picture (COP). They require timely, Combat Service Support (CSS) information to plan effectively".[17] There are two types of information categories provided in any Common Operating Picture (COP) – common and additional data files. Common data files are related to what is relevant at all levels. This information provides situational awareness and makes available to the logistician the visibility necessary to control the logistical flow. Some examples of this kind of data are Logistical Status Reports (LOGSTAR), Manifests, Distribution Matrix, Main Supply Route (MSR) and Alternate Supply Route (ASR) Status Reports, Transportation Movement Requests (TMR), Convoy Security Reports, other Critical Reports, Standard Army Management Information System (STAMIS) and Tracking information. As stated above, to create distribution, the focus is on the combination of three elements: 1) support, 2) movement, and 3) force protection. To help validate this idea, apply the common data files with the three elements. If there is any overlap between the elements, this verifies the validity of the combination of the elements in creating distribution. In addition, the importance of the common data is to provide situational awareness that is required to monitor and control the distribution pipeline.

Sustainment	+	Movement	+	Force Protection	=	Distribution
LOG REPORTING		TMR/STMR		Convoy Security Process		
Distribution Matrix		Distribution Matrix		Distribution Matrix		
Critical Reports		Critical Reports		Critical Reports		
Manifesting		Manifesting				
STAMIS		MSR/ASR Status		MSR/ASR Status		

---

[16] Ibid, 4-28.
[17] FM 3-0 (formerly FM 100-5), *Operations*. 14 June 2001, 12-6.

Additional data files are utilized to gather further information in support of the Common Operating Picture (COP) template. These files consist of but are not limited to information in conducting Mission Analysis, Queries, Commodity Inquiries, Web URLs, Documents, Diagrams, etc. Both types of data files support the Common Operating Picture (COP) template. The common data files are on a near real time feed and additional data files are required as not time, but mission sensitive.

Chapter 21

Information Management

Concept

Once the plan is complete, the hardest part then comes into effect, and that is the execution phase. If an organization or agency has prepared itself properly, then this may not be a significant emotional event. But if it has not, then the staff is in for some long days and nights. Just like in the planning phase, the organization has to clearly recognize how the primary staff and the other agencies will disseminate information and fuse data between its own organization and other agencies to maintain situational awareness, as well as a staff focus and synergy.

This is best handled with the establishment of a *Fusion Cell*, whose main purpose is to correlate, integrate, and distribute data that can provide the organization pertinent information that contributes to command and control of the operation. Therefore, the unit must establish a *process* to handle the *input* and *output* of data to facilitate information management. The process identifies the three components in the information management process consisting of the *Organizational Outlook, Organizational Information Flow,* and *Information Flow Elements.*

Theory and Execution

The first step in creating this process is to design an Organizational Outlook, which lays out the important focal points of the mission and the network and connectivity required. This structural design must be developed from the ground up, aligning the organization and its sub-agencies to establish an architecture that support the process of information management (See Figure 47; Organizational Outlook for Successful Information Management).

Organizational Outlook for Successful Information Management
1. Mission or Operation of the Unit

2. Identify the Agencies or Subordinate-Units involved
3. Categorize Expectation for Success
4. Define the Function and Process of each Unit participating: Input/Output
5. Define the Function and Method of each Unit participating: Input/Output
6. Identify Skills/Technology/Tools/Facilities required to conduct the procedure
7. Establish the Connectivity: Data, Voice, Display, Output – Network
8. Recognize and Instruct Specific Training, Techniques, and Procedures (TTP)
9. Refinement of Tools/Connectivity/TTPs to meet Mission expectation

Figure 47; Organizational Outlook for Successful Information Management

After the architecture is laid out and the users have identified the organization's mission, player expectations, method, resources, and guidance for information management, the next step is to create the Organizational Information Flow diagram. This depicts the task organization of the unit and its subordinate units that provide the network to implement procedures for an organizations staff sections and divisions to gather information from its subordinate units, as well as other agencies and to process the data input and develop data outputs to communicate to higher and subordinate units and other organizations.

As you can see from Figure 47, Organizational Information Flow, each subordinate unit and organization staff sections information input and output feeds and builds the next level of the overall organizations information management structure. The connectivity between the different staff elements, of either automation or voice output, is that established network that connects the staff entities, which supports information flow. To understand what makes up this network and the terminology utilized within the information flow architecture some important definitions need reviewing.

- Input – Consists of written or automated reports and documentation provided from lower to higher, or higher to lower within the organizations.

- Cycle – Is the sequence of events tracked either on an hourly, daily, as required timeline.

- Process – The practice a staff implements which consists of guidelines and procedures to analyze and synthesize in support of information management.

- Personnel – This category identifies those particular staff players with specific duty positions and responsibilities.

- Tool – This is what the network consists of in the area of connectivity voice or automation utilizing computers, phones, servers, network system, etc.

- Responsibility – The organization, agencies, and subunits the outputs expectations pertain too.

- Output: – Consists of written or automated reports, documentation, products, and displays provided from lower to higher, or higher to lower within the organizations.

- Content – Is the fidelity and substance of the input or output provided throughout the organization.

- Format – Guidelines, standard operating procedures (SOP) and other organizational guidance that establishes how to arrange documents, pictures, overlays, as well as live data.

- Means – The way data is displayed and/or stored, examples maybe hard copy, video feed, or network folders.

Once the information has filtered through the organization divisions and staff sections the fusion cell is the final group to evaluate, integrate, and synchronize the data (See Figure 48; Organizational Information Flow).

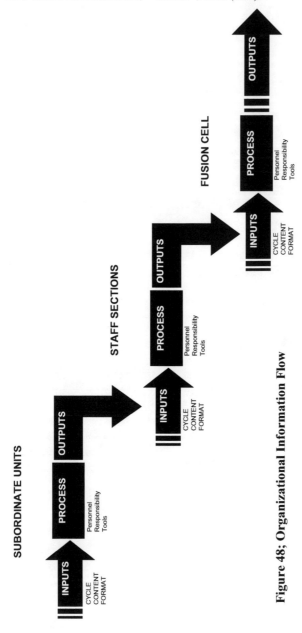

Figure 48; Organizational Information Flow

The last step in the information management process is to label key elements of the information flow process. As data, input begins to arrive into the process and the first element *"Distribution Means"* is the way that data is shared throughout the organization. The second element is the *"Target"*, which identifies the intent or objective of the mission. The third element is the most important and that is the *"Receipt Validation Agent"*, which confirms and accepts the requirement and channels the request to the right staff section or other units. The fourth element is the *"Feedback Loop"* that provides the initial information direction and guidance, by either the command section or subordinate units, required to begin staff estimates and analysis. Fifth element *"Source"* recognizes basis of the information and supplies copies of the data by the means it entered the process. The sixth element *"Inject Point"* relates to contribution between staff sections, guidance from command channels, subordinate units, and other organizations and agencies. This interjection of information, guidance, and/or data can be deliberate or incidental, the importance is that this happens before the staff analysis begins, to ensure the most current information trail is gathered. The seventh element *"Analysis"* phase begins where staff sections conduct different forms of problem solving and staff estimates to provide the organization the solution to the issue at hand. Planning section, Chapter 9 Military Decision Making Process (MDMP) can assist you in picking the best process to use to provide the best course of action. Last is the eighth element *"Dissemination Agent"* and this is simply the way the organization provides feedback to their subordinate units and other organizations providing the staff's answer and guidance. The information flow process must be put into place prior to the unit conducting real world operations so they can practice and train the staff sections, subordinate units and other organizations in the Organizational Information Flow process (See Figure 49; Information Flow Elements)

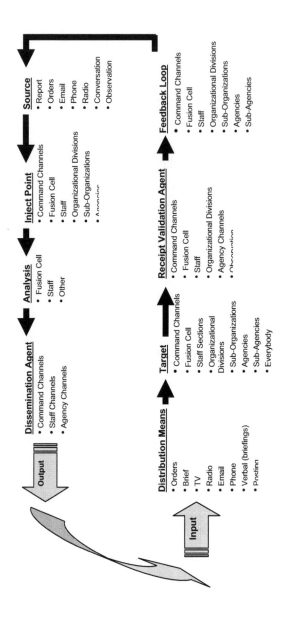

Figure 49; Information Flow Elements

Chapter 22

Establishing a Mobile Operation Center

Concept

In order to establish a mobile operation center or forward response cell you must have the proper equipment and personnel immediately available to operate the center for a 24-hour period, and be able to deploy and setup operational support in a very short timeframe. Last and most important you must be able to sustain these operations until both additional personnel are gathered and deployed to the area, and operations can move to a more stable fixed facility. These initial personnel can setup operations temporally in tents or buildings as long as they have the proper equipment to operate until the time the state and local officials can take over support operations. The following notes are some of the recourses required to establish a workable operation center or response cell that provide capabilities and results:

- Arrange for communications and power generation

- Provide for automation network feeds for computers

- Make available computers, printers, copy machines, etc.

- Supply portable tables, chairs and other furniture

- Make available office supplies (paper, pens, etc.)

- Select an area that not only your organization can setup, but your sub-organizations and other agencies can also establish their staff functions in order to facilitate information flow and coordination.

- Select sites for logistics facilities

- Set up field feeding, billeting, and shower areas

- Evaluate preventive medicine measures to determine specific support requirements (i.e. potable water)

LTC James H. Henderson, "Cotton", USA (Ret.)

Theory and Execution

There are certain elements that assist staff operations and a situational awareness of these areas consist of knowledge of basic structural design. These elements include the main operations center, separate work cells, and the type of facility used (building or tents). The key to success is an area that facilitates open discussion with briefing capability and areas for staff section, sub-organizations, and other agencies for work areas and breakout sections. The following three figures are provided for review; Figure 50, Example of building and/or tents, Figure 51, Example 1 of a Mobile Operations Center Design, and Figure 52, Example 2 of a Mobile Operations Center Design. The building and tent diagram offers room for a main operations center that is capable of seating forty-four (44) workstations on the main floor and adjacent work cell areas. The workstation furniture can be placed on portable platform risers to give the briefing area an auditorium feel that supports staff visual and communication capabilities. The main idea is to support staff synchronization and synergy within the organization.

Building

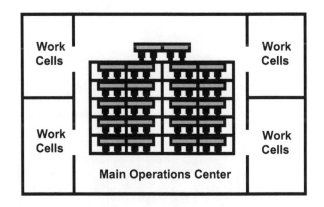

Tent

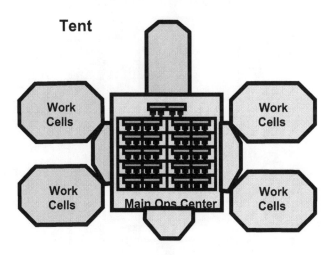

Figure 50; Example of building and/or tents

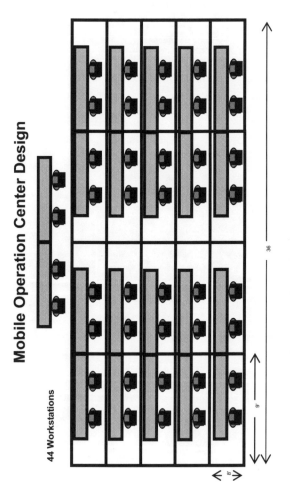

Mobile Operation Center Design

44 Workstations

Figure 51; Example 1, of a Mobile Operations Center Design

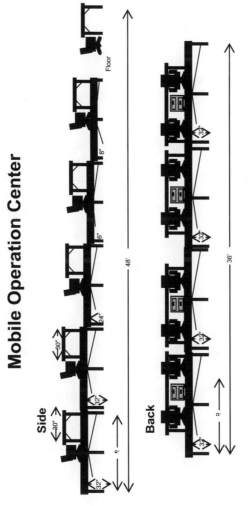

Figure 52; Example 2, of a Mobile Operations Center Design

Chapter 23

Automation

Concept

The concept of automation support to military operations refers to the use of an automated system consisting of parallel computers, workstation computers, and servers integrated within a network used to create, store, retrieve, and disseminate information. Obviously, the main purpose to automate functions within the military process is to increase quality and productivity of information, reduce time and cost, increase flexibility, eliminate human error, or make up for personnel shortage. These systems should provide the capabilities to access national level data, and provide one or more systems that continuously monitor the battlefield, directly transmit useful information throughout the different levels of war, and enable the user to request timely information from higher to lower unit organizations.

Theory and Execution

The issue is that the army does not format the system development requirements around a process. They say we want the system to do this capability, and the problem is they may not fully understand the entire process, as well as all its functions and tasked required to achieve the capability. The developers for the most part, the personnel writing the code, have never served a day in the military, and they do not completely understand the analog procedures required to successfully complete the capability required manually. The point being is that to have a workable system providing certain capabilities, the developers have to automate the manual functions and tasks within the system. For the system design to be successful, certain functions and/or tasks can be fully automated within the architecture to streamline and/or shorten the time it takes the system to complete the capabilities. The last undertaking is the integration and data sharing between the different capabilities, and the problem here is one system cannot alone conduct or correlate all the different capabilities required to support the process for example, end-to-end distribution management. There are systems of record that provide accounting functions for commodities and movement, as well as systems that record real-time information facilitating command and control (C2) and situational awareness. What is required is a platform that can integrate and share the information between the different capabilities/systems without having to place cumbersome business rules inside the different databases that corrupt the information, and make it hard for the different capabilities/systems to talk to one another.

The new concept the army is trying to develop is a services architecture that is built around different services within a website that provides different capabilities. It acquires its information and data from a collective database that is pure of business rules, functions, and tasks where the databases sole purpose is to update, share, and archive or discard the information. This concept leads me to believe then there is a requirement for these other systems providing functionally and data to the overall process. This is just a play on words, because if I understand this logic correctly, then different systems that are conducting the accounting and collection of data will ultimately become those services required to provide the information to the database, as well as conduct the queries and data analysis required to support the process. They will just migrate to a different structure to provide capabilities to an overall system of system concept.

I support the army's services concept, but I need more fidelity in the mechanics of the system operating process.
What I think is required for the concept to be relevant is:

1. the design requirements need to be based around a process, made-up of functions, which build on a series of collective tasks, and when integrated can provide capabilities that support the battle rhythm,

2. a logic base platform that can integrate and share the information between the different capabilities/systems.

For the design to be relevant and support military operations, the system must be developed around a process incorporating the pertinent logistical functions and tasks that make up the information capability required to support the logistical operational battle rhythm. In addition, the system must offer some type of logic base platform to provide an integration and data sharing capability to nest the collective functions, task, and information management processes. If we continue to build systems that do only one facet of an individual's job, and not attack the overall logistical process required, then we will continue to come up short in a collective group of systems that share data and support the total logistical automated concept. Do not get me wrong. It is not bad to do aspects of a soldier's job if those functions and task are required to complete a capability. The problem is, we have the contractors develop the function and when complete, it does not have the capability to share the data with other systems or future systems when built. We are developing software and different systems in a stovepipe process, where different government program managers and their contractors develop software and systems and are either not required or forced to work with other government program managers and their contractors so the systems can even talk to one another, heaven forbid share data. I understand contractors may not want to work with other contractors because they might have to change the way they write code, share funding on a contract, or change the way they do business. But the government has no excuses not to work together to nest the requirements, functions, tasks, and capabilities to achieve a synchronized process. Bottom line if we ever intend to develop a system or system of systems that will support the warfighter in all aspects of full spectrum operations, then we have to start now.

Summary

The above chapters have outlined some new theories, ideas, methods of execution, or maybe just a different way to look at some of the aspects of logistical support operations. I have tried to cover the majority of the different types of logistical functions, tasks, and capabilities required to develop workable process that can be incorporated into any level of war battle rhythm. As I stated before, battle rhythm is the key, the process is nested within the battle rhythm to support the overall operation. There can be more than one battle rhythm in an operation, and this is not a problem as long as they are synchronized to complement the operational outcome. Remember, the success of any logistical support operations is the quick and timely interjection of a staff battle rhythm to develop the bases for the subordinate unit's execution to be structured. Keep in mind, logistics is hard. There are too many movable parts, things to be coordinated and synchronized, but with the development of a sound battle rhythm, it can be made a little easier.

BIBLIOGRAPHY

The bibliography lists field manuals by new number followed by old number.

Joint publications

CJCSI 3121.01A. *Standing Rules of Engagement for US Forces* (U). 01 Sep.1999.

CJCSM 3113.01. *Theater Engagement Planning*. 01 Feb. 1998.

CJCSM 3500.04B. *Universal Joint Task List*. 01 Oct. 1999.

Joint Doctrine Encyclopedia. 16 Jul. 1997.

Joint Military Operations Historical Collection. 15 Jul. 1997.

JP 0-2. *Unified Action Armed Forces* (UNAAF). 10 Jul 2001.

JP 1-0. *Doctrine for Personnel Support to Joint Operations*. 19 Nov. 1998.

JP 1-02. *Department of Defense Dictionary of Military and Associated Terms*. Available online at http://www.dtic.mil/doctrine/jel/doddict/

JP 1-05. *Religious Ministry Support for Joint Operations*. 26 Aug. 1996.

JP 1-06. *Joint Tactics, Techniques, and Procedures for Financial Management During Joint Operations*. 22 Dec. 1999.

JP 2-0. *Doctrine for Intelligence Support to Joint Operations*. 09 Mar. 2000.

JP 3-0. *Doctrine for Joint Operations*. 10 Sep 2001.

JP 3-07. *Joint Doctrine for Military Operations Other Than War*. 16 Jun. 1995.

JP 3-07.1. *Joint Tactics, Techniques, and Procedures for Foreign Internal Defense* (FID). 26 Jun. 1996.

JP 3-07.2. *Joint Tactics, Techniques, and Procedures for Antiterrorism.* 17 Mar. 1998.

JP 3-07.3. *Joint Tactics, Techniques, and Procedures for Peace Operations.* 12 Feb. 1999.

JP 3-07.4. *Joint Counter drug Operations.* 17 Feb. 1998.

JP 3-07.5. *Joint Tactics, Techniques, and Procedures for Noncombatant Evacuation Operations.* 30 Sep. 1997.

JP 3-07.6. Joint Tactics, Techniques and Procedures for Foreign Humanitarian Assistance. 15 Aug 2001

JP 3-07.7. *Joint Tactics, Techniques, and Procedures for Domestic Support Operations.* TBP.

JP 3-08. *Interagency Coordination During Joint Operations.* 2 volumes. 9 Oct. 1996.

JP 3-09. *Doctrine for Joint Fire Support.* 12 May 1998.

JP 3-11. *Joint Doctrine for Operations in Nuclear, Biological, and Chemical (NBC) Environments.* 11 Jul. 2000.

JP 3-13. *Joint Doctrine for Information Operations.* 9 Oct. 1998.

JP 3-14. *Joint Doctrine for Space Operations.* TBP.

JP 3-16. *Joint Doctrine for Multinational Operations.* 05 Apr. 2000.

JP 3-18. *Joint Doctrine for Forcible Entry Operations.* TBP.

JP 3-33. *Joint Force Capabilities.* 13 Oct. 1999.

JP 3-35. *Joint Deployment and Redeployment Operations.* 7 Sep. 1999.

JP 3-53. *Doctrine for Joint Psychological Operations.* 10 Jul. 1996.

JP 3-54. *Joint Doctrine for Operations Security.* 24 Jan. 1997.

JP 3-55. *Doctrine for Reconnaissance, Surveillance, and Target Acquisition Support for Joint Operations.* 14 Apr. 1993.

JP 3-57. *Doctrine for Joint Civil Affairs.* 21 Jun. 1995.

JP 3-58. *Joint Doctrine for Military Deception.* 31 May 1996.

JP 3-59. *Joint Doctrine, Tactics, Techniques, and Procedure for Meteorological and Oceanographic Support.* 23 Mar. 1999.

JP 3-60. *Joint Doctrine for Targeting.* TBP.

JP 3-61. *Doctrine for Public Affairs in Joint Operations.* 14 May 1997.

JP 4-0. *Doctrine for Logistic Support of Joint Operations.* 06 Apr. 2000.

JP 4-01. *Joint Doctrine for the Defense Transportation System.* 19 Mar 2003.

JP 4-01.3. *Joint Tactics, Techniques, and Procedures for Movement Control.* 9 Apr. 2002

JP 4-01.4. *Joint Tactics, Techniques, and Procedures for Joint Theater Distribution.* 22 Aug. 2000

JP 4-01.7. *JTTP for Use of Intermodal Containers in Joint Operations.* 7 Jan. 1997

JP 4-01.6. *Joint Tactics, Techniques, and Procedures for Joint Logistics Over the Shore.* 12 Nov. 1998

JP 4-01.8. *Joint Tactics, Techniques, and Procedures for Joint Reception, Staging, Onward Movement, and Integration.* 13 Jun. 2000.

JP 4-02. *Doctrine for Health Service Support in Joint Operations.* 30 Jul. 2001.

JP 4-02.1. JTTP for Health Services Support Logistic Support in Joint Operations. 6 Oct. 1997.

JP 4-03. *Joint Bulk Petroleum Doctrine*. 25 Jul. 1995.

JP 4-04. *Joint Doctrine for Civil Engineering Support*. 26 Sep. 1995.

JP 4-05. *Joint Doctrine for Mobilization Planning*. 22 Jun. 1995.

JP 4-06. *JTTP for Mortuary Affairs in Joint Operations*. 28 Aug. 1996.

JP 4-07. *Joint Tactics, Techniques, and Procedures for Common User Logistics During Joint Operations*. 11 Jun. 2001.

JP 4-08. *Joint Doctrine for Logistic Support of Multinational Operations*. 25 Sep. 2002.

JP 4-09. Joint Doctrine for Global Distribution. 14 Dec. 2001

JP 5-0. *Doctrine for Planning Joint Operations*. 13 Apr. 1995.

JP 5-00.2. *Joint Task Force (JTF) Planning Guidance and Procedures*. 13 Jan. 1999.

JP 5-03.1. *Joint Operation Planning and Execution System, Volume I (Planning and Procedures)*. 04 Aug. 1993.

ARMY PUBLICATIONS

AR 71-9. Materiel Requirements. 30 Apr. 1997. Available online at http://books.usapa.belvoir.army.mil/cgi-bin/ bookmgr/BOOKS/ R71_9/CCONTENTS

DA Memo 10-1. *Executive Agent Responsibilities assigned to the Secretary of the Army*. 15 Jan. 1997.

FM 1 (FM 100-1). *The Army*. 14 Jun. 2001.

FM 1-0 (FM 12-6). *Personnel Doctrine*. 09 Sep. 94.

FM 1-04 (FM 27-100). *Legal Support to Operations*. 01 Mar. 2000.

FM 1-05 (FM 16-1). *Religious Support.* 18 Apr. 2003.

FM 1-06 (FM 14-100). *Financial Management Operations.* 07 May 1997.

FM 1-08 (FM 12-50). *U.S. Army Bands.* 15 Oct. 1999.

FM 2-0 (FM 34-1). *Intelligence and Electronic Warfare Operations.* 27 Sep. 1994.

FM 2-01.3 (FM 34-130). *Intelligence Preparation of the Battlefield.* 08 Jul. 1994.

FM 2-33.2 (FM 34-81). *Weather Support for Army Tactical Operations.* 31 Aug. 1989.

FM 3-0 (formally FM 100-5), *Operations.* 14 June 2001, 12-6.

FM 3-01.94 (FM 44-94). *Army Air and Missile Defense Command Operations.* 31 Mar. 2000.

FM 3-04.500 (FM 1-500). *Army Aviation Maintenance.* 26 Sept. 2000.

FM 3-05 (FM 100-25). *Doctrine for Army Special Operations Forces.* 01 Aug. 1999.

FM 3-05.30 (FM 33-1). *Psychological Operations.* 01 Jun. 2000.

FM 3-06 (FM 90-10). *Military Operations on Urbanized Terrain (MOUT) (How to Fight).* 15 Aug. 1979.

FM 3-07 (FM 100-19 and FM 100-20). *Stability Operations and Support Operations.* 20 Feb. 2003.

FM 3-07.2. *Force Protection.* TBP.

FM 3-07.3 (FM 100-23). *Peace Operations.* 30 Dec. 1994.

FM 3-07.6 (FM 100- 2 3). *HA_ Multi-service Procedures for Humanitarian Assistance Operations.* 31 Oct. 1994.

FM 3-07.7 (FM 100-19). *Domestic Support Operations*. 01 Jul. 1993.

FM 3-09 (FM 6-20). *Fire Support in the Air Land Battle*. 17 May 1988.

FM 3-4. *NBC Protection* (will be revised as FM 3-11.4). 29 May 1992.

FM 3-5. *NBC Decontamination* (will be revised as FM 3-11.5). 28 Jul. 2000.

FM 3-11 (FM 3-100). *Multiservice Tactics, Techniques, and Procedures for Nuclear, Biological, and Chemical Defense Operations*. 10 Mar. 2003.

FM 3-13 (FM 100-6). *Information Operations*. 27 Aug. 1996.

FM 3-14 (FM 100-18). *Space Support to Army Operations*. 20 Jul. 1995.

FM 3-16 (FM 100-8). *The Army in Multinational Operations*. 24 Nov. 1997.

FM 3-34.250 (FM 5-104). *General Engineering*. 12 Nov. 1986.

FM 3-35 (FM 100-17). *Mobilization, Deployment, Redeployment, Demobilization*. 28 Oct. 1992.

FM 3-35.1 (FM 100-17-1). *Army Pre-Positioned Afloat Operations*. 27 Jul. 1996.

FM 3-35.2 (FM 100-17-2). *Army Pre-Positioned Land*. 16 Feb. 1999.

FM 3-35.4 (FM 100-17-4). *Deployment Fort-to-Port*, 18 Jun. 2002.

FM 3-35.5 (FM 100-17-5). *Redeployment*. 29 Sep. 1999.

FM 3-55. *Reconnaissance Operations*. TBP.

FM 3-57 (FM 41-10). *Civil Affairs Operations*. 11 Jan. 1993.

FM 3-60 (FM 6-20-10). *Tactics, Techniques, and Procedures for the Targeting Process*. 08 May 1996.

LTC James H. Henderson, "Cotton", USA (Ret.)

FM 3-90. *Tactics.* 4 Jul. 2001.

FM 3-100.2 (FM 100-103-1). *ICAC2 Multiservice Procedures for Integrated Combat Airspace Command and Control.* 30 Jun. 2000 .

FM 3-100.7 (FM 100-7). *Decisive Force: The Army in Theater Operations.* 31 May 1995.

FM 3-100.11 (FM 100-11). *Force Integration.* 15 Jan. 1998.

FM 3-100.14 (FM 100-14). *Risk Management.* 23 Apr. 1998.

FM 3-100.16 (FM 100-16). *Army Operational Support.* 31 May 1995. FM 3-100.16 will be superseded by portions of FM 3-100.7 and FM 4-0 when these manuals are republished.

FM 3-100.21 (FM 100-21). Contractors on the Battlefield. 3 Jan. 2003.

FM 3-100.22 (FM 100-22). *Installation Management.* 11 Oct.1994.

FM 3-100.38 (FM 100-38). *UXO Multi-service Procedures for Operations in an Unexploded Ordnance Environment.* 10 Jul. 1996.

FM 4-0 (FM 100-10). *Combat Service Support.* 29 Aug. 2003.

FM 4-01 (FM 55-1). *Transportation Operations.* 03 Oct. 1995.

FM 4-01.4 (FM 100-10-1). *Theater Distribution.* 01 Oct. 1999.

FM 4-01.8 (FM 100-17-3). *Reception, Staging, Onward*

FM 4-01.011 (FM 55-65). *Unit Movement Operations.* 31 Oct. 2002.

FM 4-02 (FM 8-10). *Force Health Protection in a Global Environment.* 13 Feb. 2003.

FM 4-02.1. *Combat Health Logistics.* 28 Sep. 2001.

FM 4-02.6 (FM 8-10-1). *The Medical Company Tactics, Techniques, and Procedures.* 1 Aug. 2002.

FM 4-02.10. *Theater Hospitalization.* 29 Dec. 2000.

FM 4-02.17. *Preventive Medicine Services.* 28 Aug. 2000.

FM 4-02.19 (FM 8-10-19). *Dental Service Support in a Theater of Operations.* 1 Mar. 2001.

FM 4-20 (FM 10-1). *Quartermaster Principles.* 11 Aug. 1994.

FM 4-30.2 (FM 9-43-1). *Maintenance Operations and Procedures.* 1 Sep. 2000.

FM 4-30.11 (FM 21-16). *Unexploded Ordnance (UXO) Procedures.* 30 Aug. 1994.

FM 4-30.12 (FM 9-15). *Explosive Ordnance Disposal Service and Unit Operations.* 08 May 1996.

FM 4-30.13 (FM 9-13). *Ammunition Handbook,* 1 Mar. 2001.

FM 4-30.16. *Explosive Ordnance Disposal of Multiservice Procedures for EOD in a Joint Environment,* 15 Feb. 2001.

FM 4-93.4 (FM 63-4). *Theater Support Command.* 15 Apr. 2003.

FM 4-93.51 (FM 63-21-1). *Tactics, Techniques, and Procedures for the Division Support Battalion.* 26 May 2002.

FM 4-93.53 (FM 63-21-1). *Tactics, Techniques, and Procedures for the Division Aviation Support Battalion.* 2 May 2002.

FM 4-100.2 (FM 100-10-2). *Contracting Support on the Battlefield.* 04 Aug. 1999.

FM 4-100.9 (FM 100-9). *Reconstitution.* 13 Jan. 1992.

FM 5-0 (FM 101-5). *Staff Organizations and Operations.* 31 May 1997. When revised, FM 5-0 will be renamed Planning.

FM 5-100. *Engineer Operations* (will be revised as FM 3-34). 27 Feb. 1996.

FM 5-116. *Engineer Operations: Echelon above Corps* (will be revised as FM 3-34.211). 9 Feb. 1999.

FM 6-0. *Command and Control.* TBP.

FM 6-22 (FM 22-100). *Army Leadership.* 31 Aug. 1999.

FM 7-0 (FM 25-100). *Training the Force.* 22 Oct. 2002.

FM 7-10 (FM 25-101). *Battle Focused Training.* 30 Sep. 1990.

FM 7-15. *Army Universal Task List (AUTL).* TBP.

FM 8-10-6. *Medical Evacuation in a Theater of Operations Tactics, Techniques, and Procedures* (will be revised as FM 4-02.2). 14 Apr. 2000.

FM 8-10-18. *Veterinary Services Tactics, Techniques, and Procedures* (will be revised as FM 4-02.18). 22 Aug. 1997.

FM 8-42. *Combat Health Support in Stability Operations and Support Operations* (will be revised as FM 4-02.42). 27 Oct. 1997.

FM 8-51. *Combat Stress Control in a Theater of Operations* (will be revised as FM 4 02.51). 29 Sep. 1994.

FM 8-55. *Planning for Health Service Support* (will be revised as FM 4-02.55). 9 Sep. 1994.

DEPARTMENT OF DEFENSE PUBLICATIONS

DOD Directives available online at http://web7.whs.osd.mil/corres.htm

DOD *Civil Disturbance Plan, Annex C (Concept of Operations),Appendix 8 (Special Instructions),* 15 Feb. 1991; modified by Director of Military Support message 161639Z Jul. 96, *Subject: Changes to DOD Civil Disturbance*

DODD 1315.6. *Responsibilities for Military Troop Construction Support of the Department of the Air Force Overseas.* 26 August 1978

DODD 2310.1. DOD Program for Enemy Prisoners of War (POW) and Other Detainees. 18 August 1994

DODD 3025.15. *Military Assistance to Civil Authorities*. 18 Feb. 1997.

DODD 3100.10. *Space Policy*. 09 Jul. 1999.

DODD 4140.25. *DOD Management Policy for Energy Commodities and Related Services*. 20 April 1999

DODD 4500.9. *Transportation and Traffic Management*. 26 January 1989

DODD 4525.6. *Single Manager for Military Postal Service.*, 5 May 1980

DODD 4705.1. *Management of Land-Based Water Resources in Support of Joint Contingency Operations*. 9 July 1992

DODD 5030.49. *DOD Customs Inspection Program*. 6 January 1984

DODD 5100.1. *Functions of the Department of Defense and its Major Components*. 1 August 2002

DODD 5160.65. *Single Manager for Conventional Ammunition (SMCA)*. 8 March 1995
DODD 5100.1. *Functions of the Department of Defense and Its Major Components*. 1 Aug. 2002.

DODD 5100.46. *Foreign Disaster Relief*. 4 Dec. 1975.

DODD 5160.54. *Critical Asset Assurance Program (CAAP)*. 20 Jan. 1998.

DODD 5525.5. *DOD Cooperation with Civilian Law Enforcement Officials*. 15 Jan. 1986.

DODD 5500.7. *Standards of Conduct*. 30 August 1993

DODD 5515.8. *Single Service Assignment of Responsibility for Processing of Claims*. 9 June 1990

DODI 4140.50. *Management of DOD Locomotives*. 9 December 1982

DOD Memo. *Mortuary Affairs*

"*DOD Principles of Information.*" Washington, D.C.: Government Printing Office, 01 Apr. 1997. Available online at http://www/defenselink.mil/admin/about.html#PrinInfo

National Military Strategy of the United States of America, 1997. Available online at http://www.dtic.mil/jcs/nms

NATO MCD 319/1. *NATO Principles and Policies for Logistics* (http://www.nato.int)

NATO MCD 389. *Combined Joint Task Force Concept* (http://www.nato.int)

PUBLIC LAWS AND OTHER PUBLICATIONS

The United States Code is available online at http://uscode.house.gov/usc.htm

AAFES Reg 8-4. *Army and Air Force Exchange Service Regulation*

AAFES Reg 8-6. *Army and Air Force Exchange Service Operating Procedures*

AJP 4. *Allied Joint Logistic Doctrine*

ALP 4.2. *Land Forces Logistics*

ALP 9. *Land Forces Logistics Doctrine*

Arms Export Control Act (Public Law 90-629, Oct. 22, 1968, [82 Stat. 1320]; see Title 22 USC, section 2751, Short Title note).

Authority to Use Army and Air National Guard in Certain Counter-drug Operations (Title 32 USC, section 112).

CGSCM 3500.04B. Universal Joint Task List, Version 4.0. 01 Oct. 1999.

Civil Military Cooperation Action Program (Title 10 USC, section 401).

Defense Against Weapons of Mass Destruction Act of 1996 (Public Law 104-201, section xiv [110 Stat. 2422]). Available online at http://www.access.gpo.gov/nara/publaw/104publ.html

Federal Acquisition Regulation. Sep. 2001.

Federal-Aid Highway Act of 1956, Creating the Interstate System: Public Roads, v. 60, no. 1, http://www.tfhrc.gov/pubrds/summer96/p96su10.htm

Federal Response Plan. Available online at http://www.fema.gov/r-n-r/frp

Foreign Assistance Act of 1961 (Public. Law 87-195, Sept. 4, 1961, [75 Stat. 424]; see Title 22 USC, section 2151, Short Title note).

Goldwater-Nichols Department of Defense Reorganization Act of 1986 (Title 10 USC, Subtitle A, Part I, Chapter 5). Available online at http://dtic.mil/jcs/core/title_10.html

Joint Vision 2010 (Washington, DC: Joint Chiefs of Staff, 1995), 24. Insurrection Act (Title 10 USC, Chapter 15).

Military Support for Civilian Law Enforcement Agencies (Title 10 USC, sections 371-382, Chapter 18).

National Security Act of 1947 (61 Stat. 495, chapter 343; see Title 50 USC, section 401, Short Title note).

National Security Decision Directive 221, Narcotics and National Security, 08 Apr. 1986.

Posse Comitatus Act (Title 18 USC, section 1385).

SECDEF Memo. *Veterinary Support*: Oct. 1990.

SECDEF Memo. *Joint Mortuary Affairs Program.*

ST 9-11-X. *Army Automation Support Procedures.*

Title 10 USC, Annex B, section 3013 (responsibilities of the secretary of the Army).

GLOSSARY

Abbreviations and Acronyms

AAFES   Army & Air Force Exchange Service

AALPS   Automated Air Load Planning System

ACITVS   Army CONUS ITV Server

ADCON   Administrative Control

AES   Automated Export Shipper System

AFKS   Air Force Knowledge Service

AIS   Automated Information Systems

AJP   Allied Joint Publication

AMC   Army Material Command

AMS   Automated Manifest System

AMS-TAC   Automated Manifest System- Tactical

AO   Area of Operation

APOD   Air Port of Debarkation

APOE   Aerial Port of Embarkation

APS   Aerial Port Squadron

ARTCMD   Army Trans Control Movement Doc

ARTEP   Army Training and Evaluation Program

ASL   Authorized Stockage List

ASP   Ammunition Supply Points

ASR   Alternate Supply Route

ATCMD   Advance Transportation Control Movement
           Document

ATLASS   Asset Tracking, Logistics and Supply System

AUTL   Army Universal Task List

BCS3   Battle Command Sustainment Support System

BCT	Brigade Combat Team
BDE	Brigade
BDE	Brigade
BN	Battalion
BSB	Brigade Sustainment Battalion
C2	Command and Control
CAEMS	Computer-Aided Embarkation
CALM	Computer-Aided Load Manifesting Center
Carriers	Commercial Freight Carriers
CAS	Combat Ammunition System
CAV	Cavalry
CBAT	Capabilities-Based Analysis Team
CCDR	Combatant Commander
CDR	Commander
CEO	Chief Executive Officer (corporate title)
CFA	Call Forward Area
CHE	Container Handling Equipment
CMOS	Cargo Movement Operations System
CO	Company
COA	Course of Action
COCOM	Combatant Command
COMPASS	Computerized Movement Planning and Status System
COMSEC	Communications Security
CONOPS	Concept of Operations
CONUS	Continental United States
COP	Common Operating Picture
CPP	Convoy Protection Platform
CPX	Command Post Exercise

CSS	Combat Service Support
CSSB	Combat Service Support Battalion
CTC	Cargo Transfer Company
CULT	Common User Land Transportation
D2C2	Deployment and Distribution and Command and Control
DBSMC	Defense Business Systems Management Committee
DCTS	Defense Collaboration Tool Suite
DDOC	Deployment and Distribution Center
DEL	Deployment Equipment Lists
DEPORD	Deployment Order
DFAS	Defense Finance/Accounting System
DFWG	Distribution Functional Working Group
DISA	Defense Information Systems Agency
DISN	Defense Information Systems Network
DLA	Defense Logistics Agency
DM	Distribution Management
DMB	Distribution Movement Board
DMC	Distribution Management Center
DMT	Distribution Management Teams
DOD	Department of Defense
DOS	Days of Supply
DPfM	Distribution Portfolio Management
DPO	Distribution Process Owner
DRO	Domestic Route Order
DRR	Domestic Routing and Rating
DSN	Defense Switching Network
DSS	Distribution Standard System

eMILPO	Electronic Military Personnel System
ESC	Expeditionary Sustainment Command
ETR	Export Traffic Release
ETRR	Export Traffic Release Request
EXORD	Execution Order
FACTS	Financial and Air Clearance Transportation
FARE	Forward Area Refueling Equipment
FAWPSS	Forward Area Water Point Supply System
FB	Football
FBCB2	Force XXI Battle Command Brigade and Below
FEDLOG	Federal Logistics Catalog
FL	Forklift
FM	Field Manual
FOB	Forward Staging Bases
FOC	Full Operational Capability
FSC	Forward Support Company
FSSP	Fuel System Supply Point
FST	Forward Surgical Team
GATES	Global Air Transportation Execution System
GDSS	Global Decision Support System
GEO	Geographic
GFM	Global Freight Management
GRP	Group
GTN	Global Transportation Network
HEMTT	Heavy Expanded Mobility Tactical Truck
HMMWV	High-Mobility Multipurpose-Wheeled
HN	Host Nation
HNA	Host Nation Agreement

HRT	Highway Regulation Teams
HRT	Highway Regulating Team
IBS	Integrated Booking System
IBS-CMM	IBS-Container Management Module
IC3	Integrated Command, Control, and Computers
ICODES	Integrated Computerized Deployment System
ICT	Institute for Creative Technologies
IM	Information Management
IO	Information Operations
IP	Internet Protocol
IRB	Investment Review Board
IRRIS	Intelligent Rail-Road Information Server
ISB	Intermediate Staging Base
ISR	Intelligence, Surveillance and Reconnaissance
ITAP-DB	Integrated Total Army Personnel Database
ITO	Installation Transportation Office
ITV	In-Transit Visibility
IWS	Info Work Space
JDL	Joint Data Library
JFC	Joint Forces Commander
JFRG II	Joint Forces Requirements Generator
JP	Joint Publications
JRSOI	Joint Reception, Staging, Onward Movement and Integration
JTF-PO	Joint Task Force – Port Opening
LAN	Local Area Network
LMR	Land Mobile Radio
LMSR	Large Medium Speed Roll on / Roll off

LMTV   Light Medium Tactical Vehicles 4x4 Trucks

LNO   Liaison Officer

LOC   Logistical Lines of Communication

LOG   Logistical

LOGAIS   Logistics Automated Information System

LOGMOD   Logistics Module

LOGSA   Logistics Support Activities

LOGSTAR   Logistical Status Reports

LOS   Line-of-Sight

LSA   Logistical Support Area

MAC II   Mission Assurance Category II

MAGTF   Marine Air-Ground Task Force

MAGTF II   Marine Air-Ground Task Force War
             Planning System II

MANPER-B   Manpower Personnel Module Base

MCB   Movement Control Battalion

MCT   Movement Control Team

MDMP   Military Decision Making Process

MDSS II   Marine Air-Ground Task Force Deployment
             Support System II

METS II   Military Export Traffic System II

MHE   Material Handling Equipment

MILVAN   Military-Owned Demountable Container

MPOC   Mobile Port Operations Center

MRO   Material Release Order

MRR   Maintenance Readiness Report

MSC   Military Sealift Command

MSCO   Military Sealift Command Offices

MSOC   Mobile Sealift Operations Center

MSR	Main Supply Route
MTS	Mobile Tracking Systems
MTV	Medium Tactical Vehicles
MURP	Munitions Report
NATO	North Atlantic Treaty Organization
NCFMIS	Naval Construction Force Management Information System
NCO	Non-Commissioned Officer
NFL	National Football League
NIPRNET	Non-Secure Internet Protocol Router Net
NTC	National Training Center
OCONUS	Overseas Continental United States
ODIM	Over Dimensional
OIF	Operation Iraqi Freedom
OP	Operational
OPCON	Operational Control
OPNS	Operations
OPS	Operations
OTO	One Time Only
PAX	Passengers
PBUSE	Property Book Unit Supply-Enhanced
PDK	Portable Deployment Kit
PIC	Positive Inbound Clearance
PLS	Palletized Loading System
POD	Port of Debarkation
POL	Petroleum, Oils, and Lubricants
PSA	Port Support Activity
RDD	Required Delivery Date
RDECOM	Army Research, Development, and

Engineering Command

REPOL	Reporting Emergency Petroleum, Oils, and Lubricants
RFF	Request for Forces
RFI	Radio Frequency Interference
RFID	Radio Frequency Identification Devices
RF-ITV	Radio Frequency In-Transit Visibility
RFS	Request for Services
RIP	Relief in Place
RO / RO	Roll on / Roll off
ROE	Rules of Engagement
ROLMS	Retail Ordnance Logistics Management System
RON	Rest Over Night Sites
ROWPU	Reverse Osmosis Water Purification Unit
RSO	Reception, Staging, and Onward Movement
RSO&I	Reception, Staging, Onward Movement, and Integration
RT	Rough-Terrain
RTFL	Rough-Terrain Forklift
SAR	Satellite Access Requests
SARSS	Standard Army Retail Supply System
SATCOM	Satellite Communications
SATS	Standard Asset Tracking System
SBSS	Standard Base Supply System
SC (E)	Sustainment Command (Expeditionary)
SC(E)	Sustainment Command (Expeditionary)
SDDC	Strategic Deployment and Distribution Command
SECDEF	Secretary of Defense

SECDEF	Secretary of Defense
SIDPERS	Standard Installation Division Personnel System
SIPRNET	Secret Internet Protocol Router Network
SMC	Surface Movement Center
SMFT	Semi Trailer-Mounted Fabric Tank
SOP	Standard Operating Procedure
SP	Starting Point
SPM	Single Port Manager
SPO	Support Operations Officer
SPOD	Sea Port of Debarkation
SSA	Supply Support Activities
SSA	Supply Support Activity
ST	Strategic Theater
STAMIS	Standard Army Management Information Systems
STEP	Standardized Tactical Entry Point
STON	Short Ton
STRATIS	Storage, Retrieval, Automated Tracking Integrated System
STTC	Simulation and Training Technology
SUS	Sustainment
SUS BDE	Sustainment Brigade System
TAA	Tactical Assemble Area
TAV	Total Asset Visibility
TB	Technical Bulletin
TCACCIS	Transportation Coordinators' Automated Command and Control Information System
TC-AIMS II	Transportation Coordinators' - Automated Information for Movements System II

TDD	Time Definite Delivery
TDM	Theater Distribution Management
TEMPER	Tent, Expandable, Modular, Personnel
TEU	Twenty-foot Equivalent Units
TMR	Transportation Movement Request
TOA	Transition of Authority
TOC	Tactical Operation Center
TPFDD	Time-Phased Force Deployment Data
TRACKER	Transportation Reconciliation and Certification Tool
TRANSEC	Transmission Security
TSC	Theater Support Command
TTP	Trailer Transfer Points
TTP	Training, Techniques, and Procedures
UD/MIPS	Unit Diary, Marine Integrated Personnel System
UDL	Unit Deployment List
UHF	Ultra High Frequency
UJTL	Universal Joint Task List
ULLS-S4	Unit Level Logistics System-S4
ULN	Unit Line Number
UMO	Unit Movement Officer
US	United States
USJFCOM	Unites States Joint Forces Command
USM	University of Southern Mississippi
USTRANSCOM	United States Transportation Command
UTC	Unit Type Code
VHF	Very High Frequency

VSAT	Very Small Aperture Terminal
VTC	Video Teleconferencing
WARNO	Warning Order
WMD	Weapons of Mass Destruction
WPS	World-wide Port System

ABOUT THE AUTHOR

Lieutenant Colonel James H. Henderson was commissioned a 2d Lieutenant and assigned to the Quartermaster following completion of his Master's Degree from the University of Southern Mississippi in May 1985. He is also a graduate of the United States Army Command and General Staff College, the Quartermaster Officer Basic Course and Quartermaster Officer Advanced Course.

Lieutenant Colonel Henderson has severed tours in Operations Desert Shield and Storm, as well as Operations Iraqi Freedom II (OIF II). He retired from active duty on 1 August 2005, and is now working as a consultant for the Army's logistical automation systems the Battle Command Sustainment Support System (BCS3) and the Transportation Coordinators-Automated Information for Movements System II (TC-AIMS II). Mr. Henderson is the author of, *The Process of Military Distribution Management; A Guide to Assist Military and Civilian Logisticians in Linking Commodities and Movement, and Logistics in Support of Disaster Relief.* He conducts classes and seminars for the U.S. Army Quartermaster and Transportation Schools, as well as instructs National Guard and Reserve units on Distribution Management and Logistical Support to Disaster Relief at Camp Shelby, Mississippi.

Acknowledgements

My deepest thanks go to Julia and Matt from the Institute for Creative Technologies (ICT), Bill of Quicksilver Software, Inc., and Chris of Stranger Entertainment whom over the passed two years have had a great impact on fueling the fire for the foundation of this book, and having received their generous advice and support this book has benefited greatly.